YOU

VISIT

RELAX

EXPLORE

IMAGINE

WRITE

THINK

DRAW

ART

BE

U

_____

YOUR NAME GOES ON THIS LINE

WORK

PLAY

PASSION

. . .

_____

_____

_____

. .

.

EXPLORE • IMAGINE • WRITE • DISCOVER • DRAW

NORTHWEST FLORIDA

another day in Destin

draw something in this box

JIM CLARK

. . .

NOTES FOR WRITING YOUR BOOK
what will your book's name be? will it be fiction or non-fiction? will it be
your life story of fame and fortune or a romantic love story? start writing

_____

_____

_____

_____

_____

_____

_____

This book is a work of creative fun for me, hopefully a little work/reward for you,
and your personal piece of art to share with others. Here are some of the people
who helped make it happen through motivation, memories, and thoughts in my
head. Not in any specific order and if you don't see your name it's not because
I don't love you. Mara, Taylor, Lindsey, Mom, Dad, Jack, Gisele, Diego, Daryl,
all my family, Jake, Marvin, Bri, Nicole, Facebook friends, Cindy, Lana, Winston,
Bridget, Dill, Mary, Maryanne, eBoo, Candy, Rae, ad3 friends, and last but not
least, you too.

Copyright © 2015 by Jim Clark
NORTHWEST FLORIDA... another day in Destin
www.nwfla.com

Editor ~ Mara Rodriguez Layout/Design by Clark & Company ~ www.juststay.com
Cover Photo by Jim Clark | Back Cover Image by Gisele Martinez

ISBN: 978-1-329-75136-1

ENJOY PHOTOGRAPHY

THINK ABOUT STUFF

WRITE WORDS DOWN

SPACES TO DRAW ON

CREATE ART TO SHARE

time to think and doodle outside the box

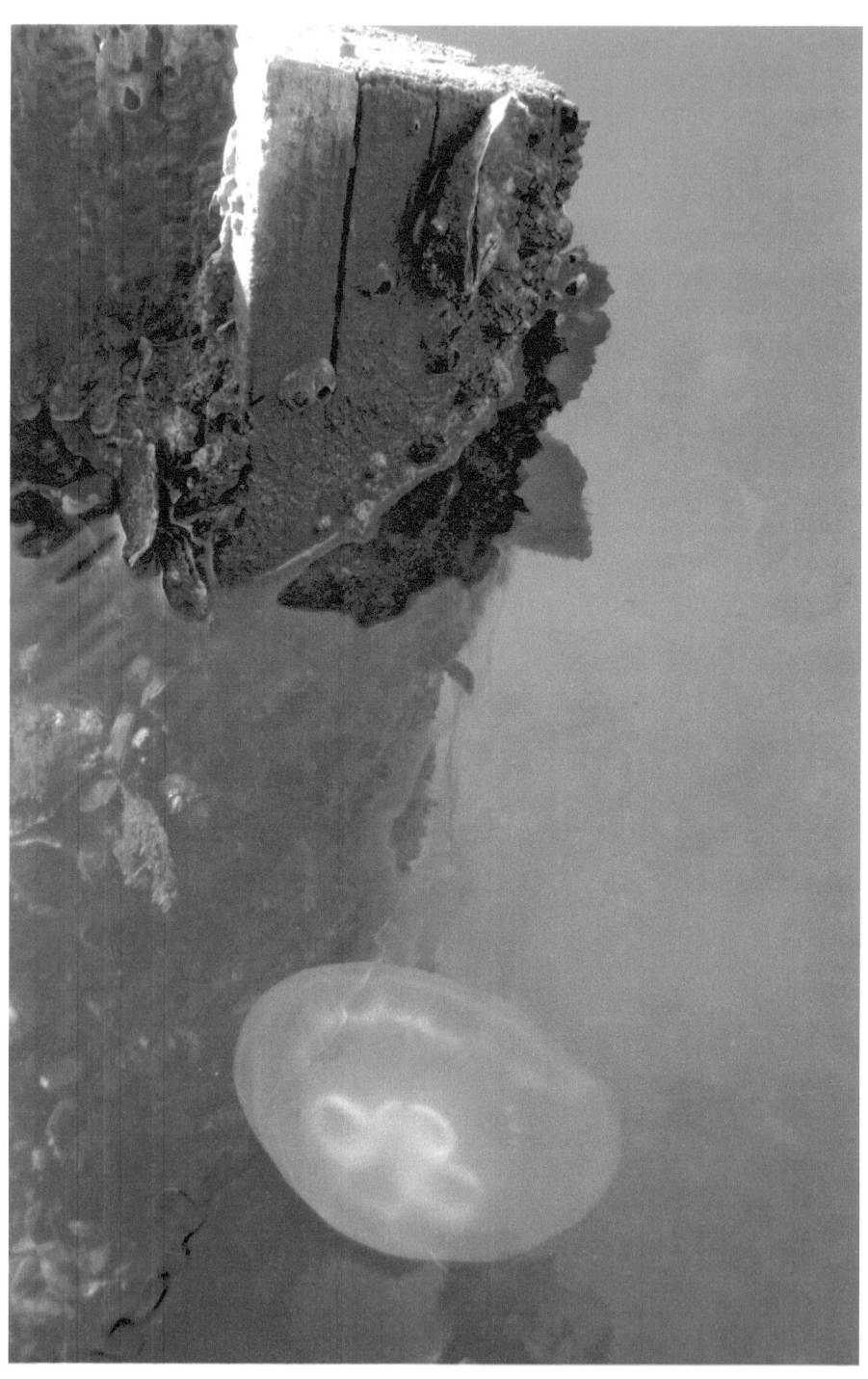

"I STILL HAD TO TOUCH IT"

INTRODUCTION

blah blah blah... this book is going to be about you not me. start writing
your introduction here. my name is _____ and here's
a few things you might like to know about me.

_____

_____

_____

_____

_____

_____

_____

_____

_____

DEDICATION

why did I do this? I put this little book together to share my photos with
people as well as to give them the opportunity to learn something about
themselves. writing or drawing can help you look inside yourself and
explore things you haven't thought about lately or ever at all. you might
just enjoy looking at the photos of the Destin area, beaches, and wildlife.
that's ok too.

who are you going to share your book with? write their names down here

_____

_____

_____

_____

_____

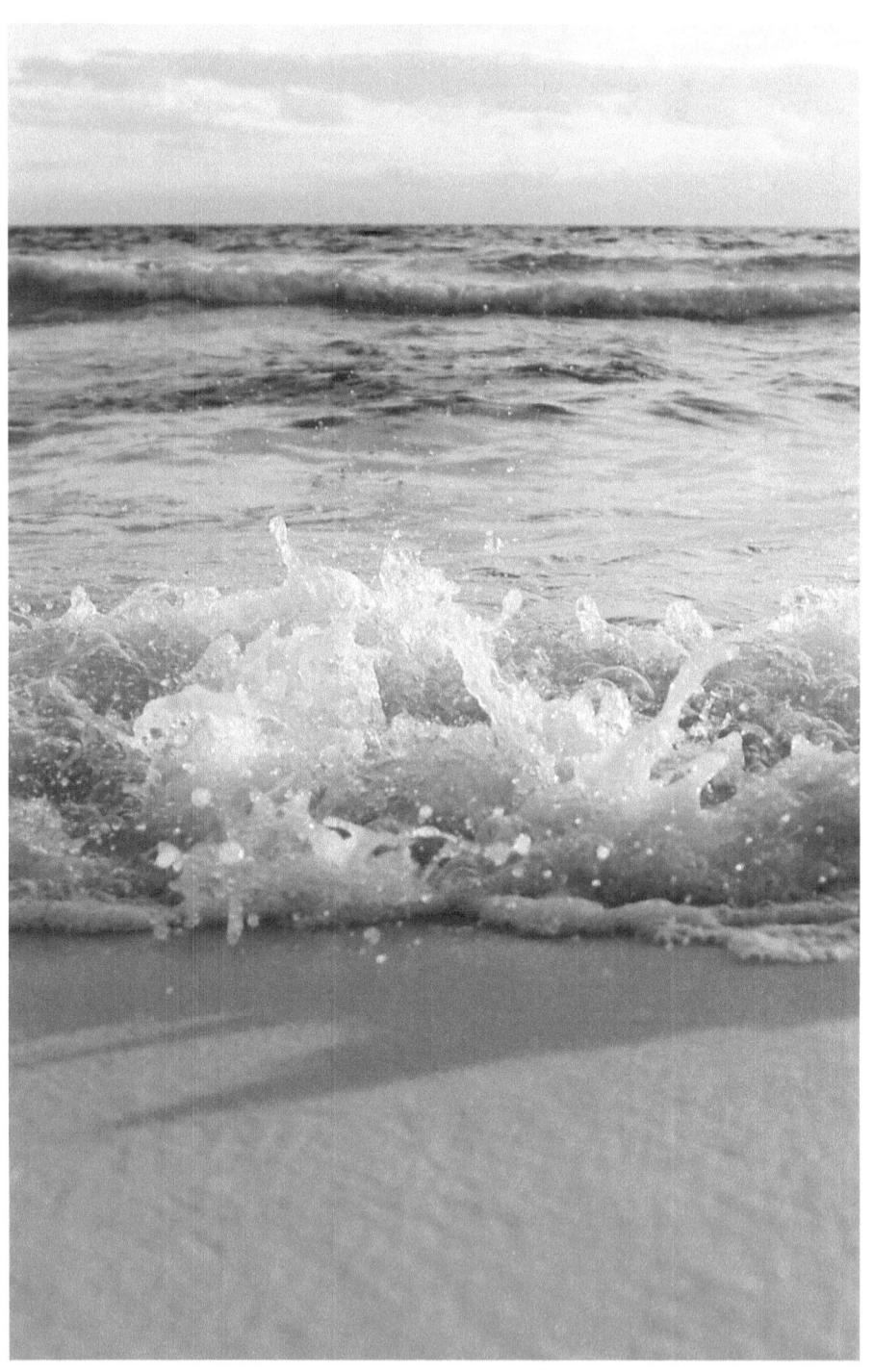

"HOW'S THE WATER?"

HOW DOES THIS WORK?

well, it's your book now so you can do whatever you want with it. you can write in it, draw in it, tape stuff on it, compose your thoughts, and anything else your heart desires. do it and then share it with others.

I hope you take time to enjoy the photos in the book as much as i enjoyed taking them. remember the good times at the beach, maybe even the bad times, because we all learn from our mistakes, right? hopefully we do or did or will someday soon. you only have one life so live it to its fullest.

_____

_____

_____

_____

_____

_____

_____

_____

_____

_____

_____

_____

_____

_____

_____

_____

_____

_____

_____

_____

NORTHWEST FLORIDA... another day in Destin

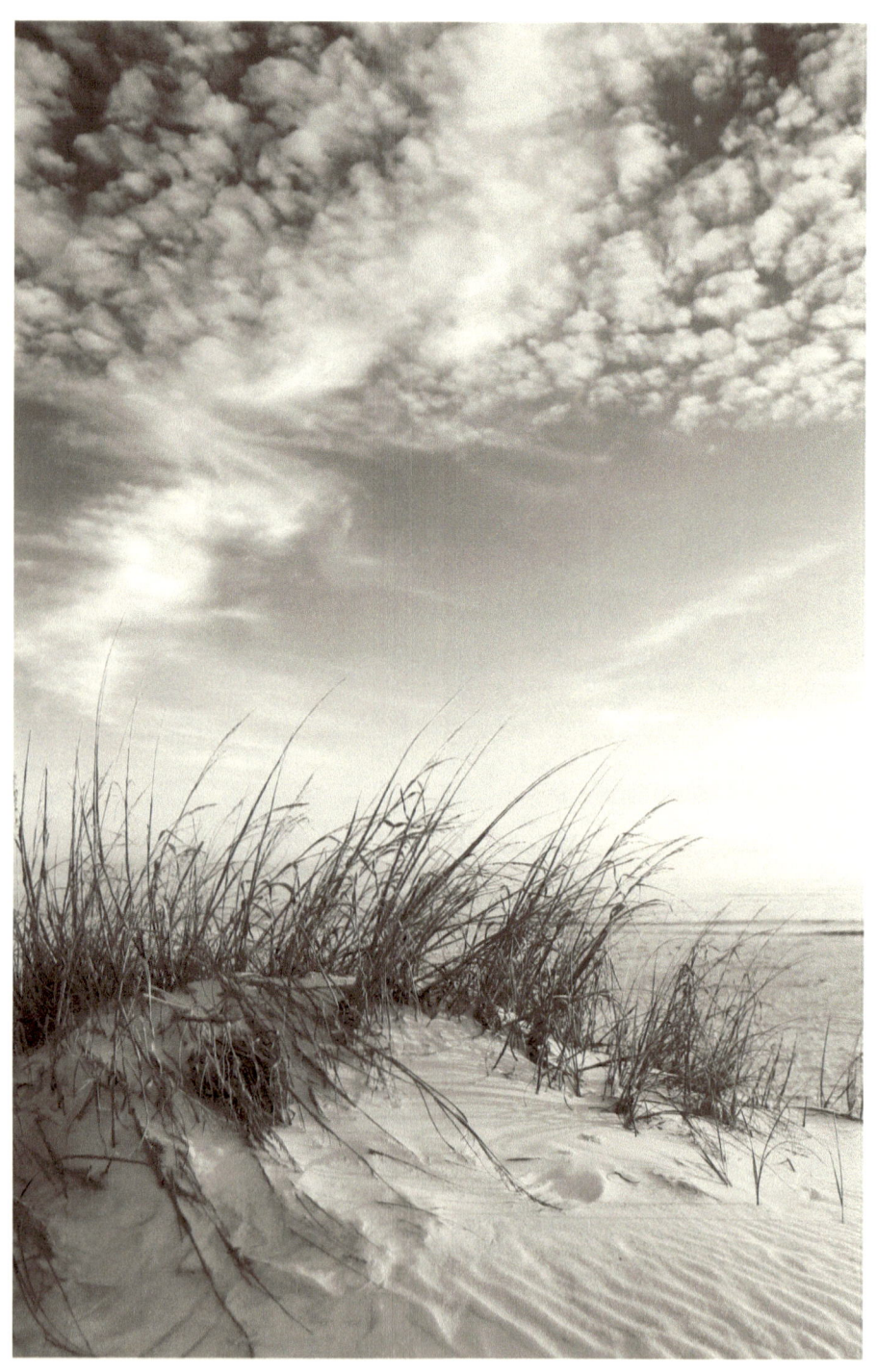

"UNDER THE CLOUDS"

WHAT'S ON YOUR MIND?

are you relaxed or stressed? get it all out and on paper

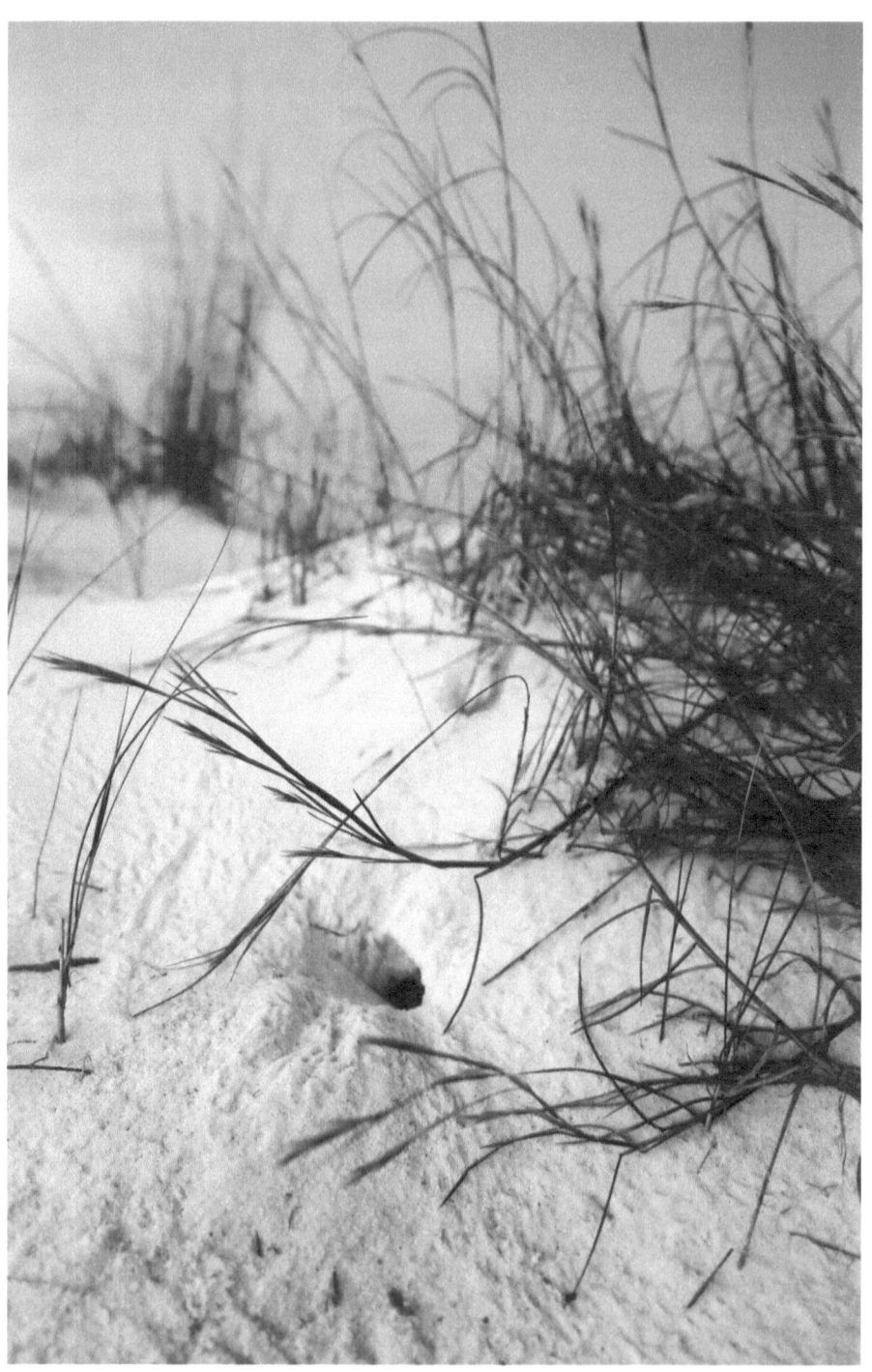

"CRAB HOLE"

WHERE DO YOU GO TO ESCAPE?

get away from the real world, people, or things

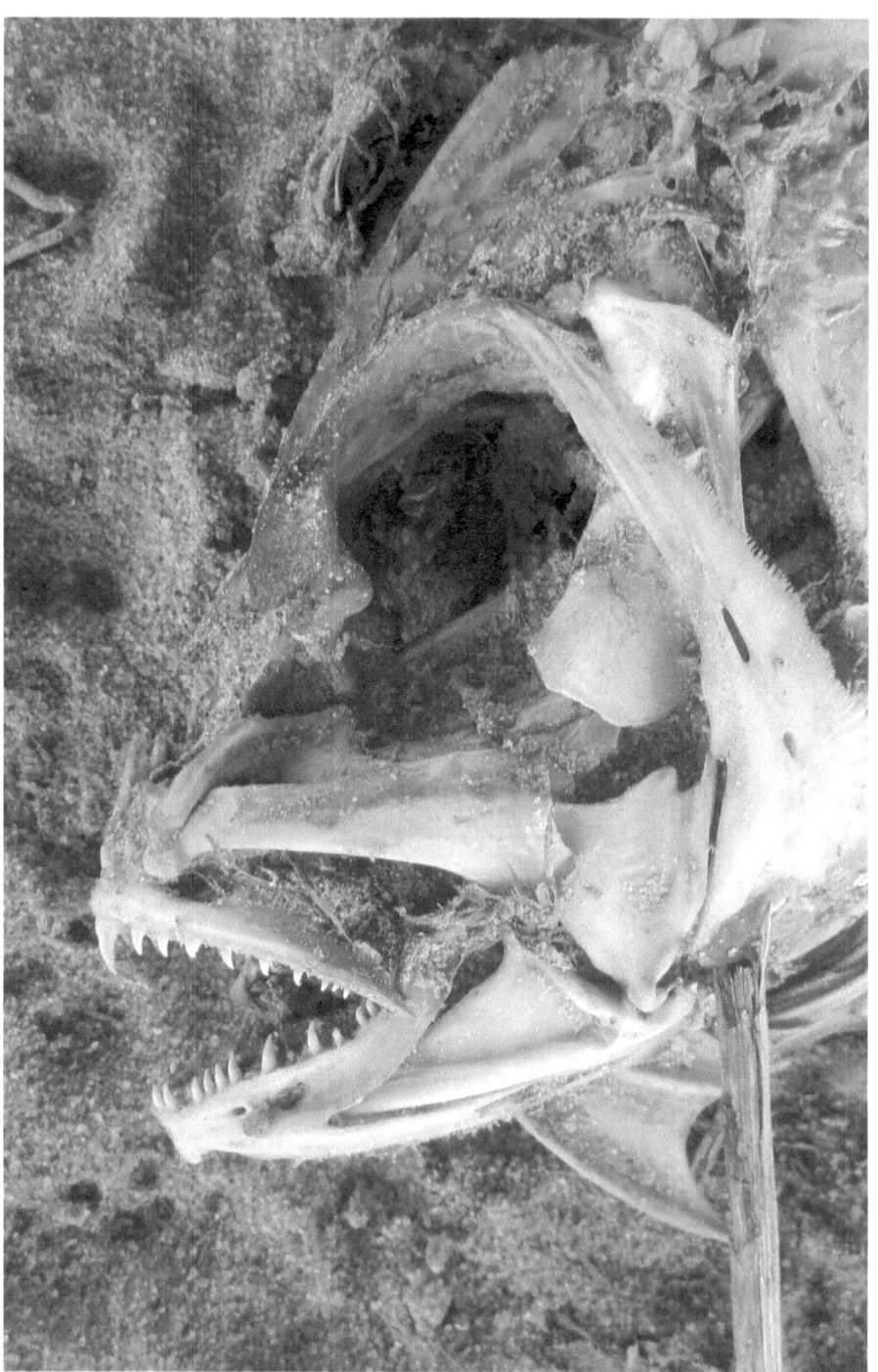

"TOOFIES"

WHAT'S YOUR BEST FEATURE?
your cheek bones, lips, eyes, or feet? ha ha ha

_____

_____

_____

_____

_____

_____

_____

_____

_____

_____

_____

_____

_____

_____

_____

_____

_____

_____

_____

_____

_____

_____

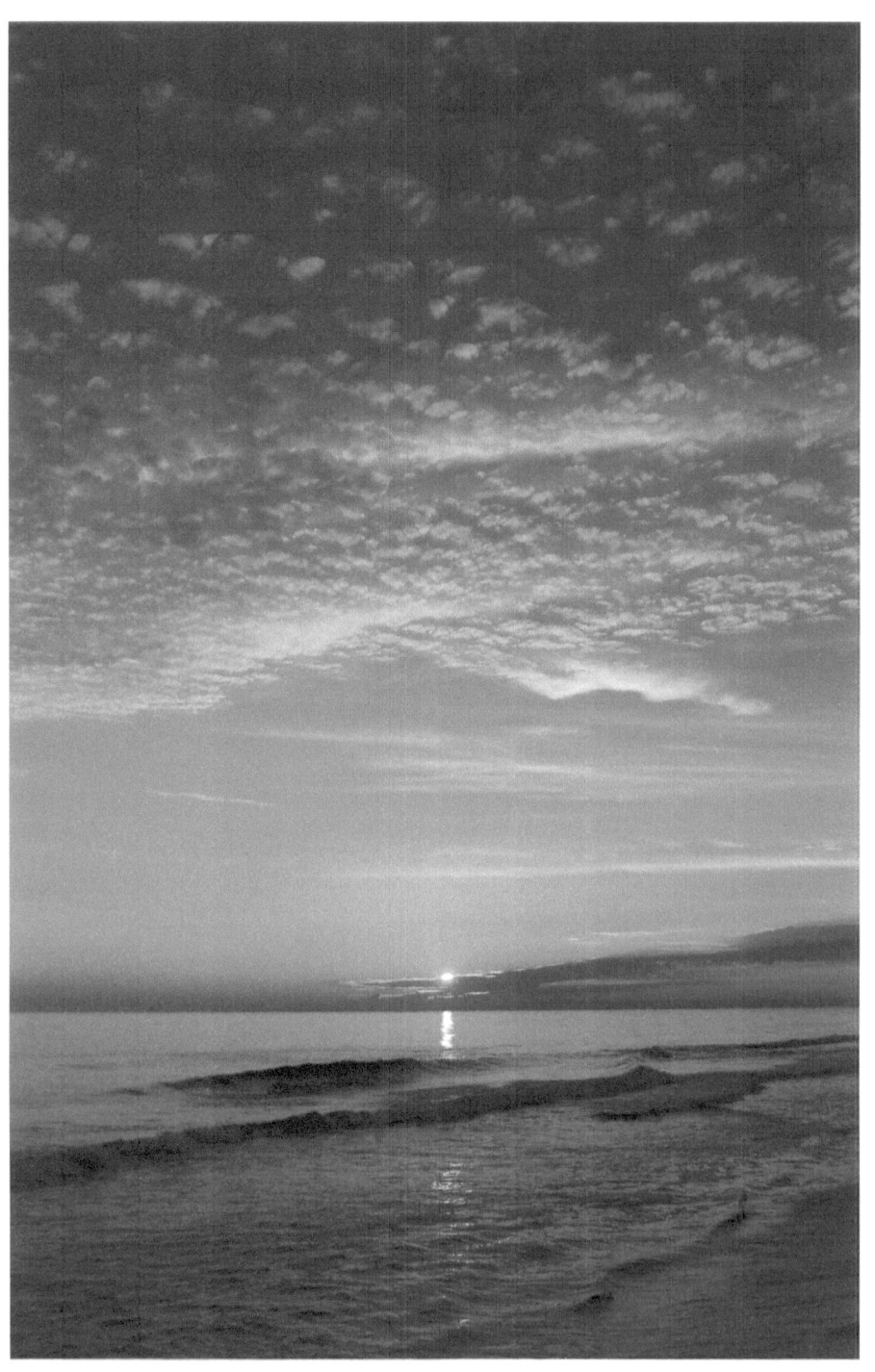

"WAVE GOODBYE TO THE SUNSET"

IF THIS WAS YOUR LAST SUNSET...
what would you do? who would you say goodbye to?

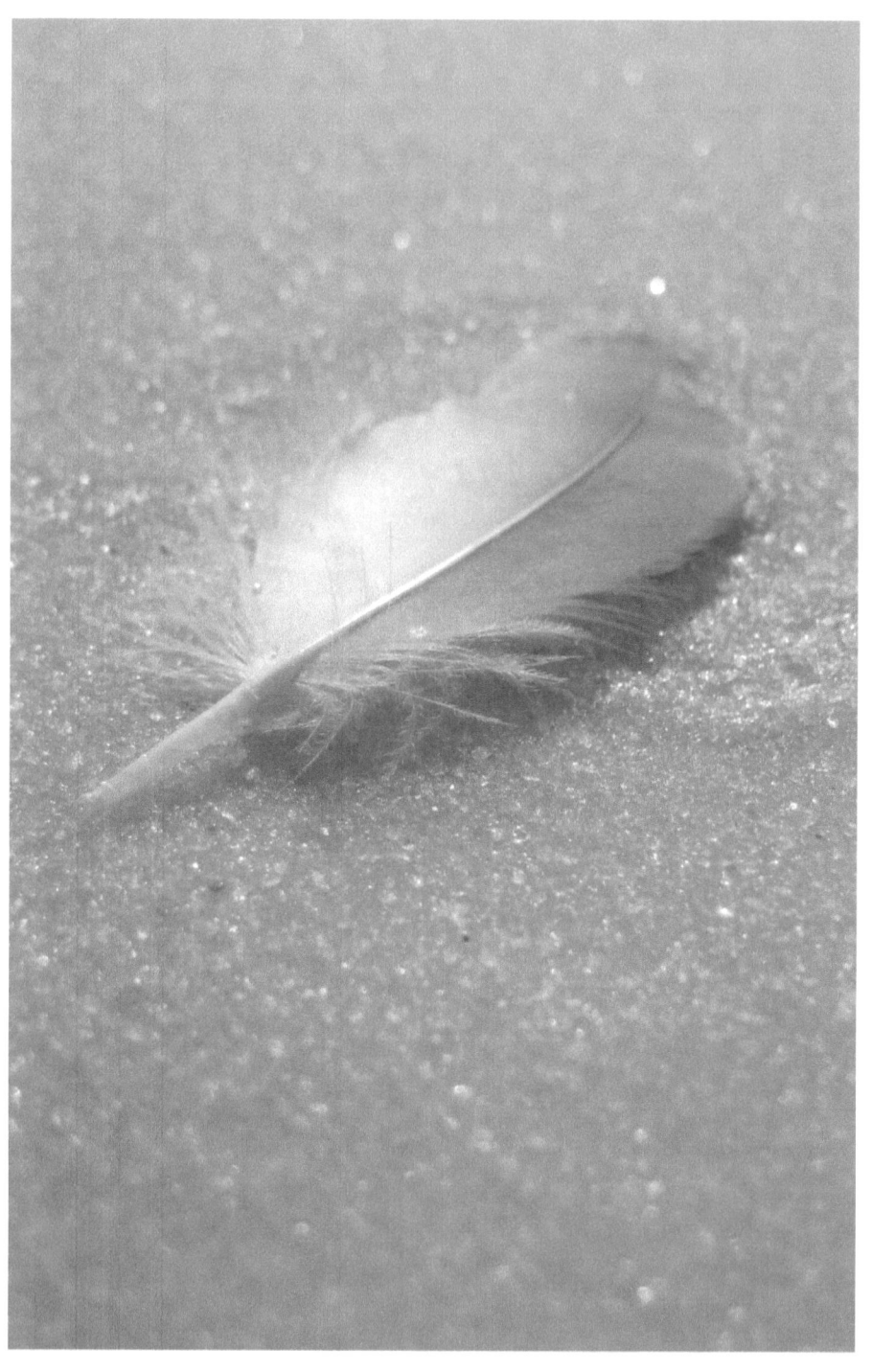

"AS LIGHT AS"

LIGHT AS A FEATHER

if you were, where would the wind take you?

_____

_____

_____

_____

_____

_____

_____

_____

_____

_____

_____

_____

_____

_____

_____

_____

_____

_____

_____

_____

_____

_____

_____

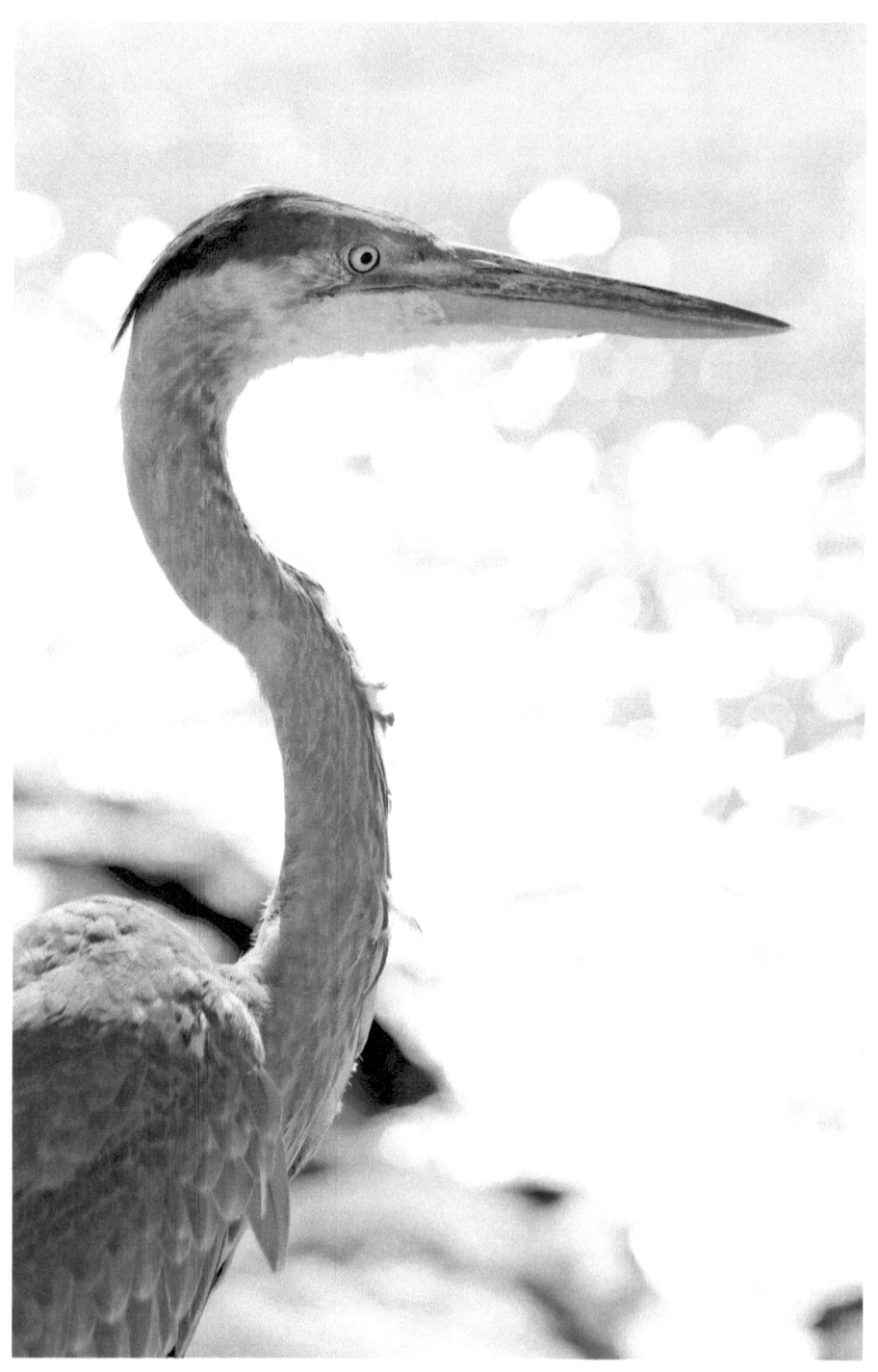

"YOU DON'T SEE ME"

WHAT'S YOUR SUPER POWER?
if you had one... mine is to turn invisible at will

NORTHWEST FLORIDA... another day in Destin

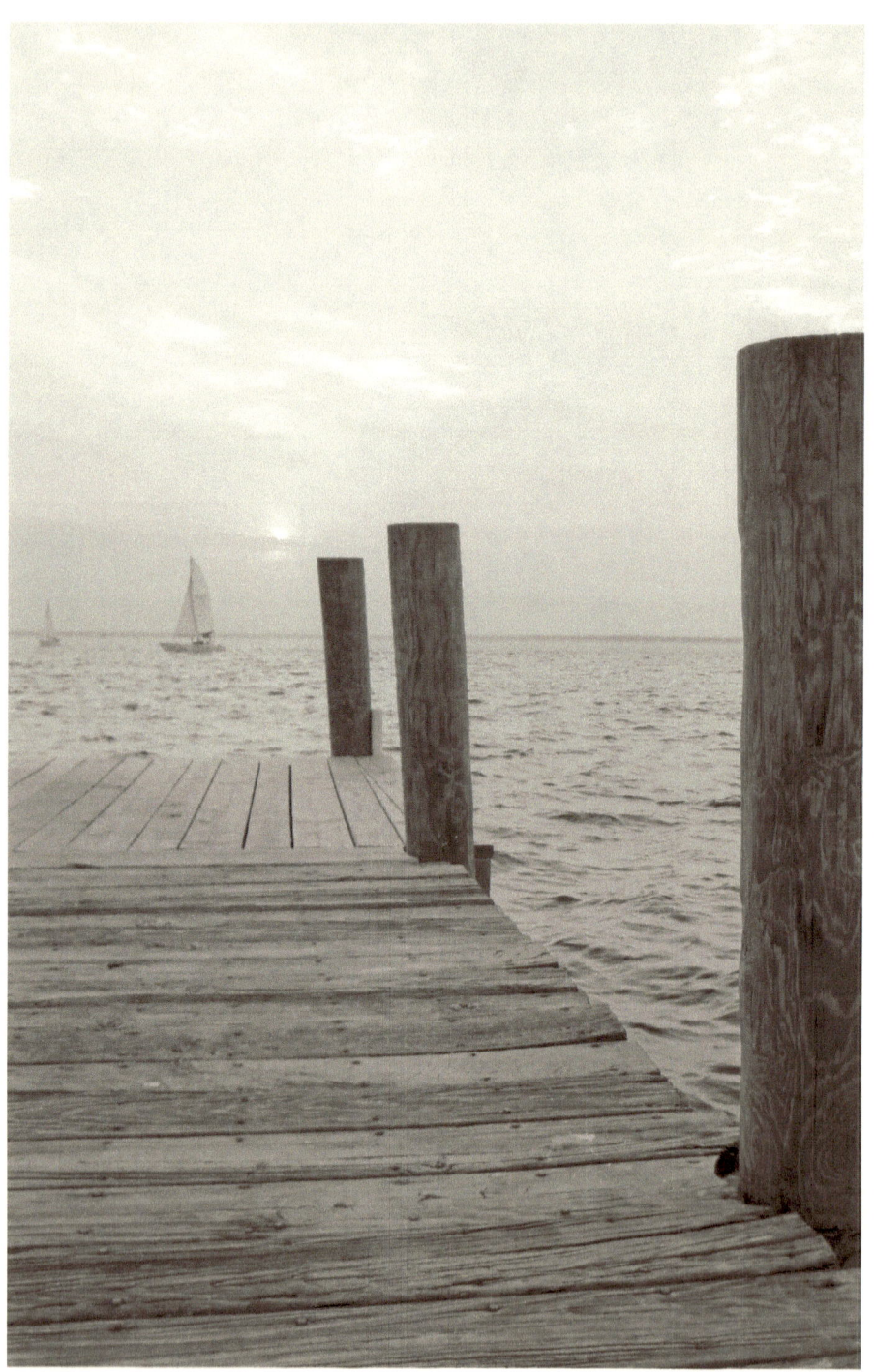

"THINKING ABOUT SITTING"

WHAT ARE YOUR FAVORITE SONGS?
from today, your childhood, or a long time ago. what genre are they?

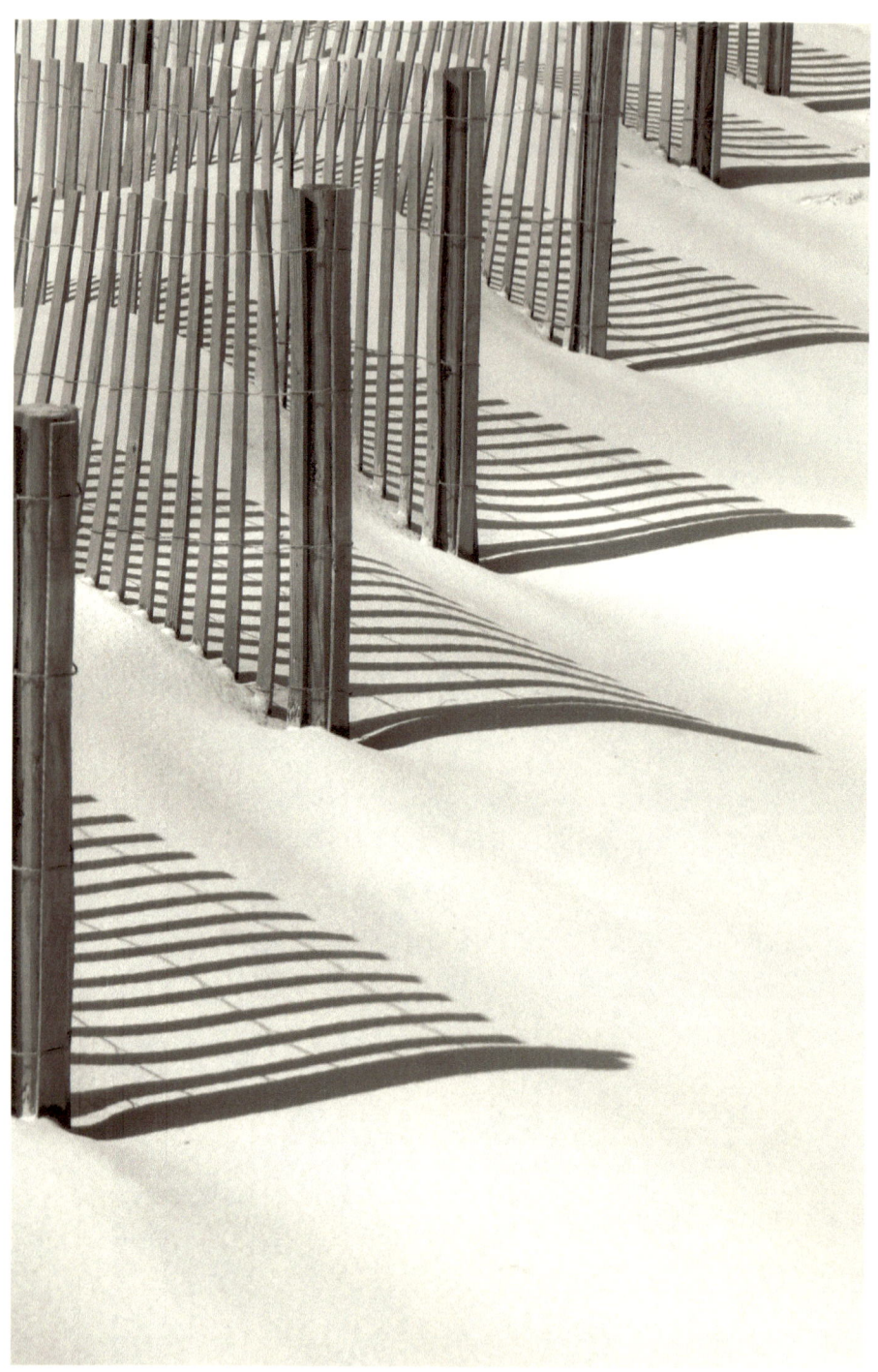

"SAVE THE DUNES"

HOW MANY STRIPES DO YOU SEE?

do you like those kinds of games? write whatever you like

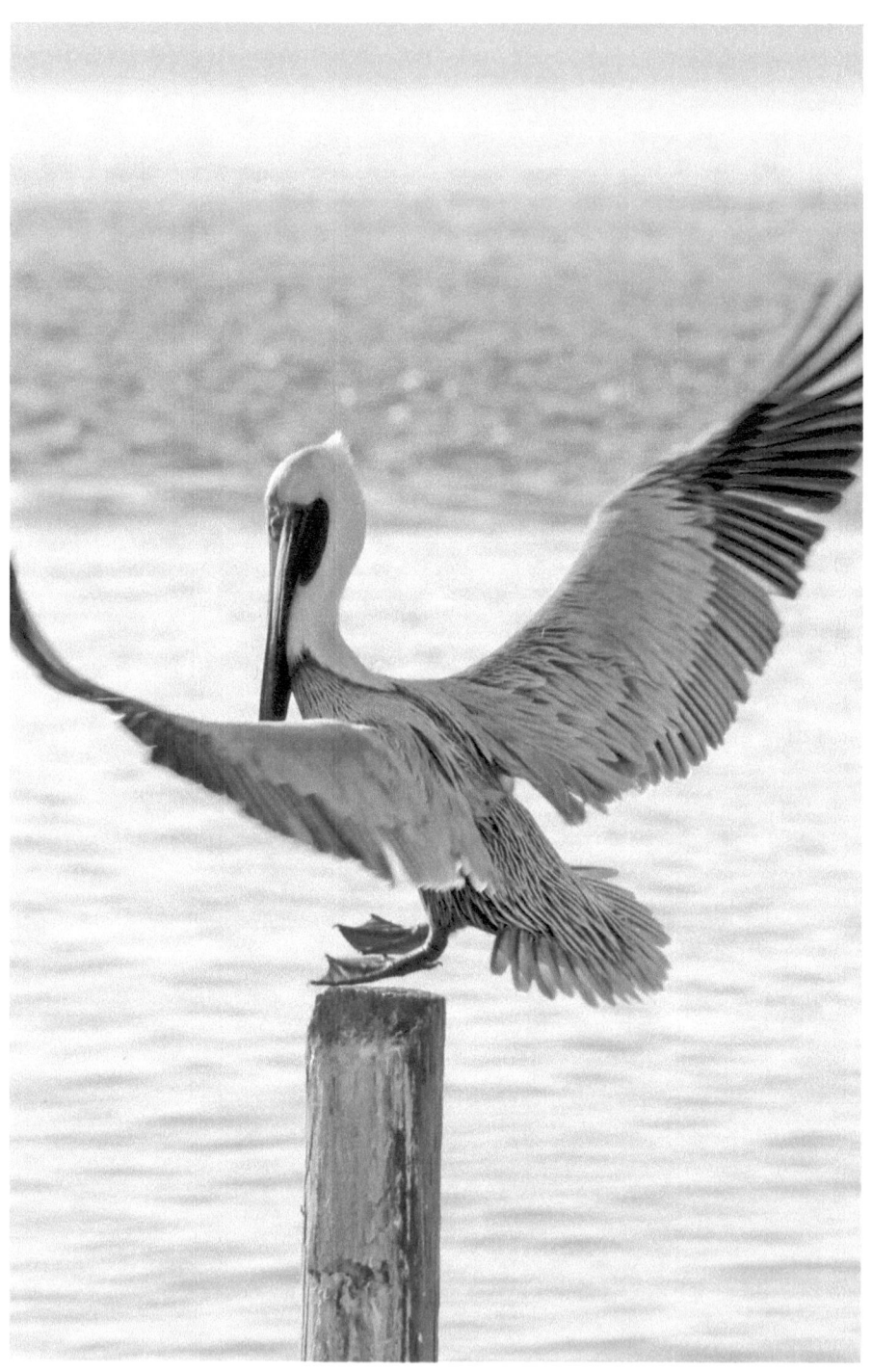

"I GOT THIS"

HAVE YOU EVER BEEN SCARED?
did you get over it? did you learn anything from it?

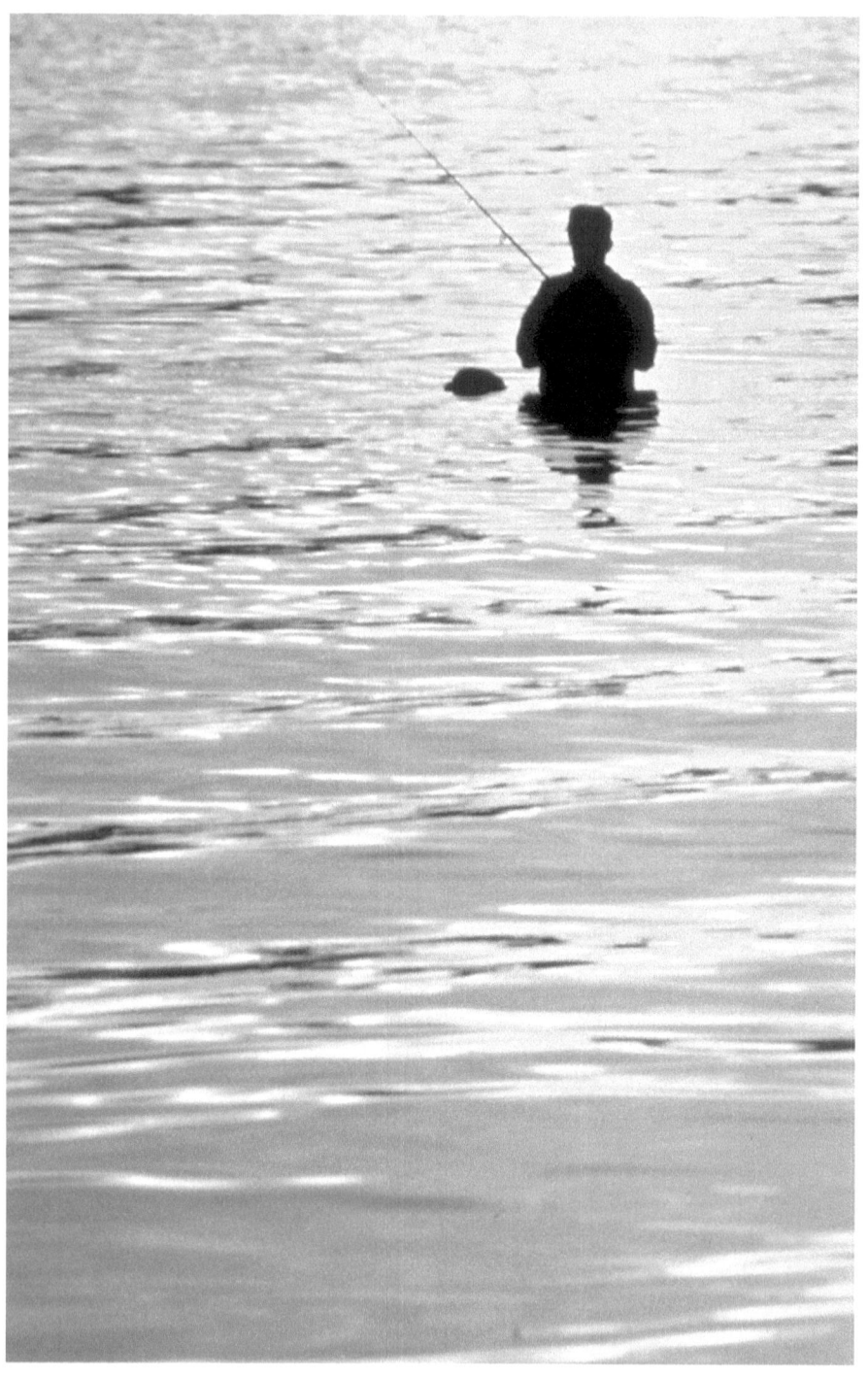

"TROUT FISHING"

DRAW THE FISH HE CAUGHT

is it big or small? with or without teeth? draw scales, fins, fishy stuff, and
maybe even give it a name too

_____

_____

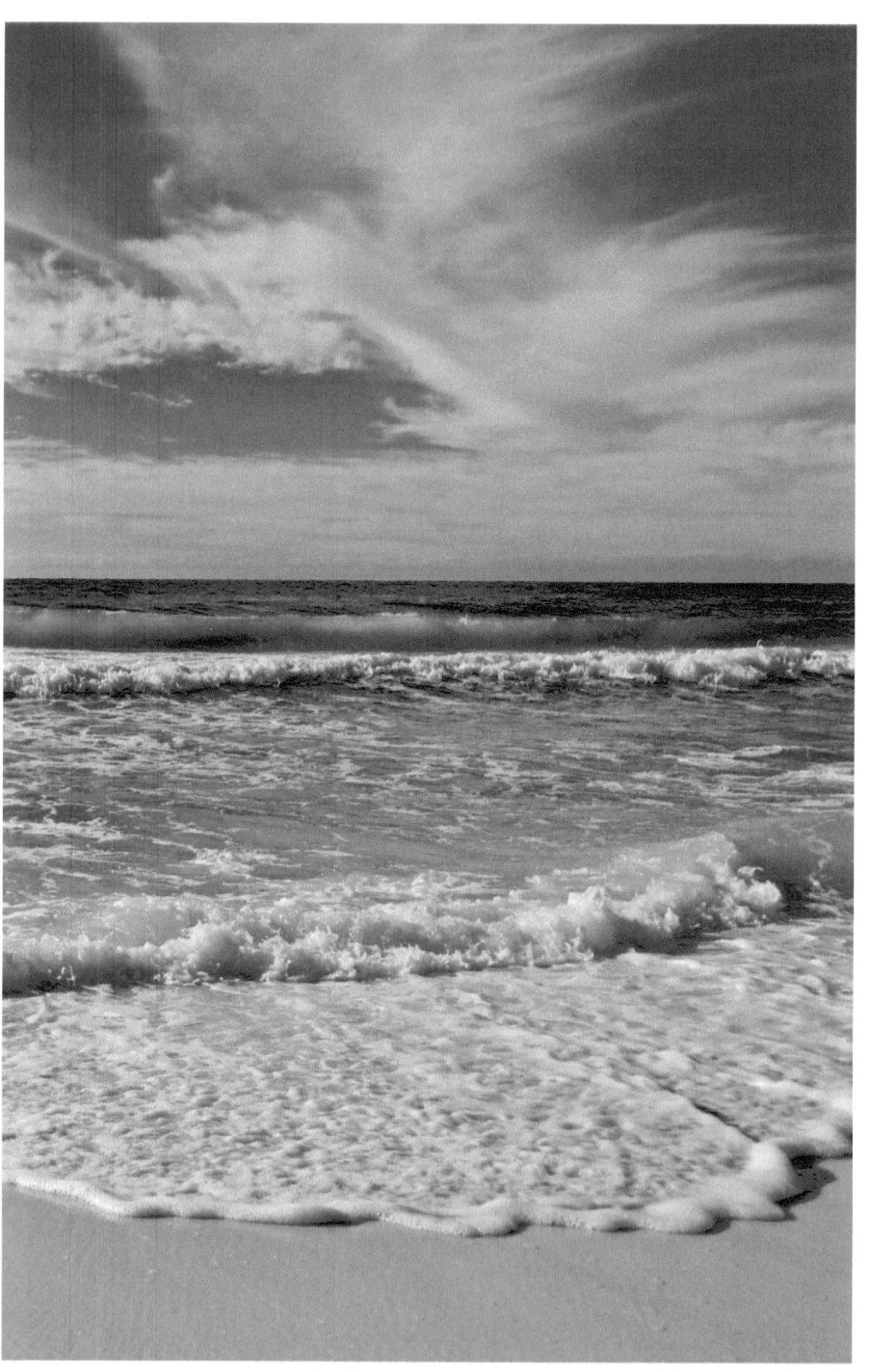

"MAKING BUBBLES"

THE DESTINATION OR THE JOURNEY?
we all have heard it before... write what you think it is

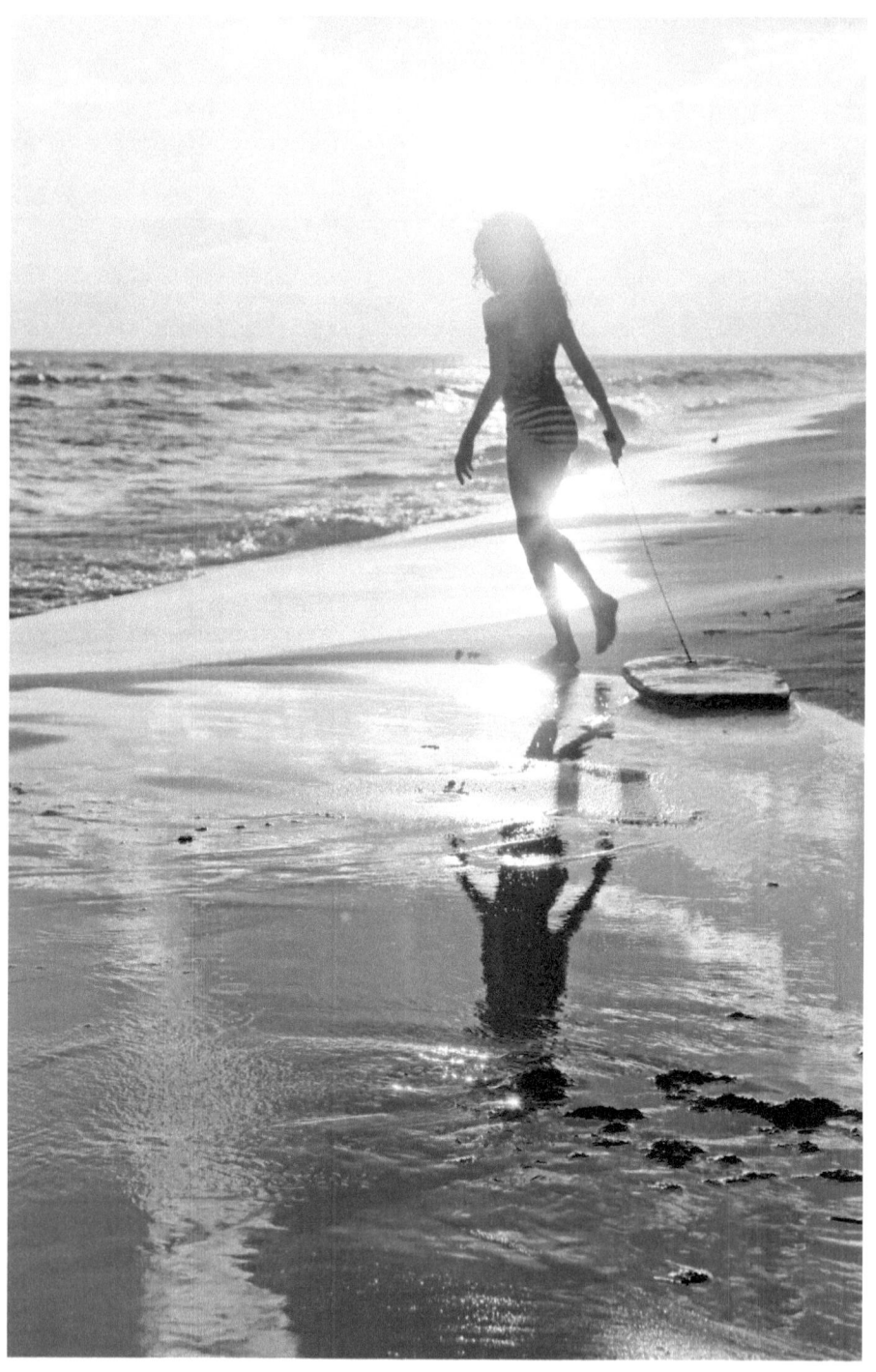

"FUN AT SUNSET"

BETWEEN YOUR TOES

describe how the sand, water, sun, and wind feels...

_____

_____

_____

_____

_____

_____

_____

_____

_____

_____

_____

_____

_____

_____

_____

_____

_____

_____

_____

_____

_____

_____

NORTHWEST FLORIDA... another day in Destin

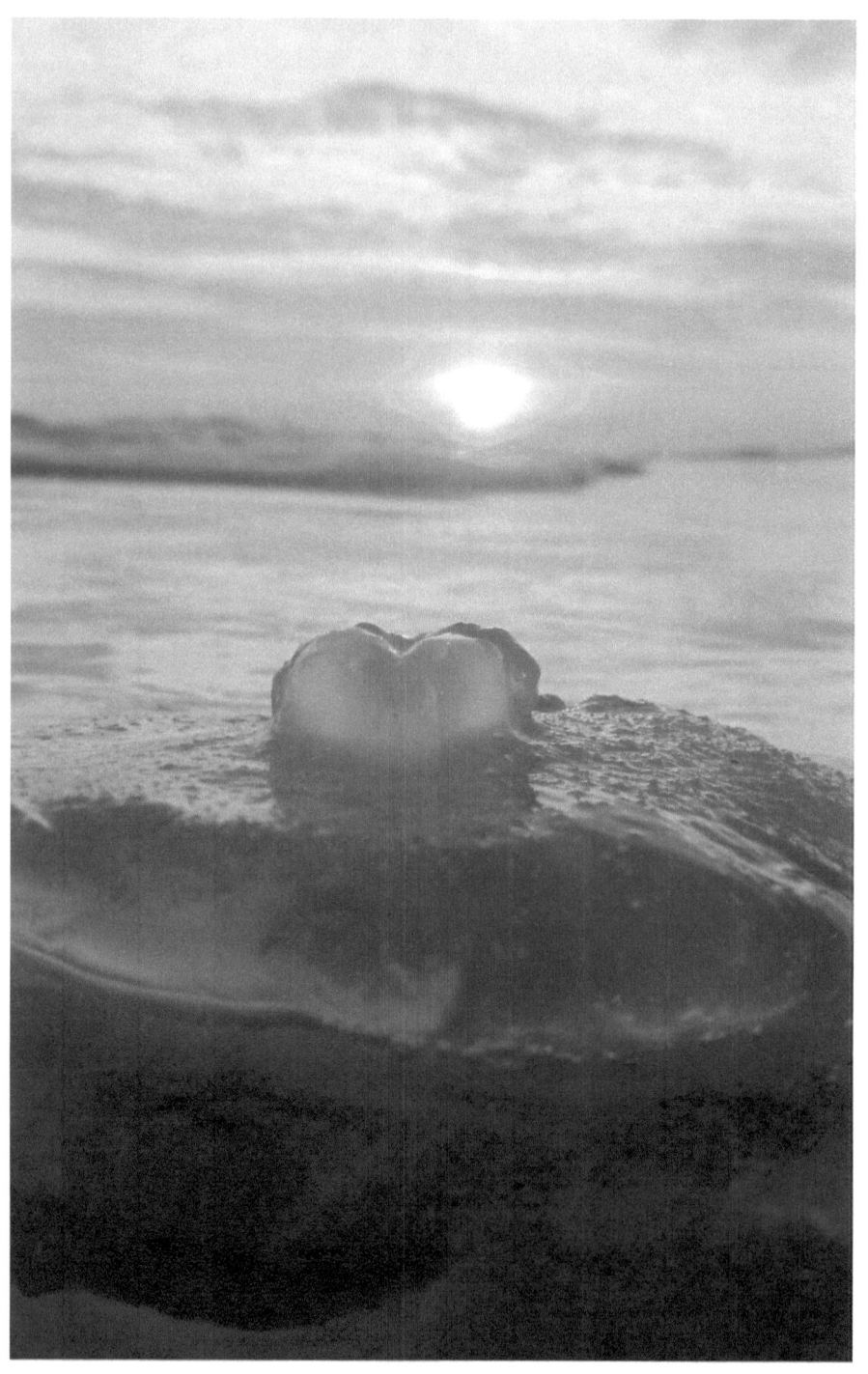

"SHARE THE LOVE"

LOVE IS FOREVER?
when you fall in love for the first time you think it will last forever, right?
write names of people, places, or things you love or loved

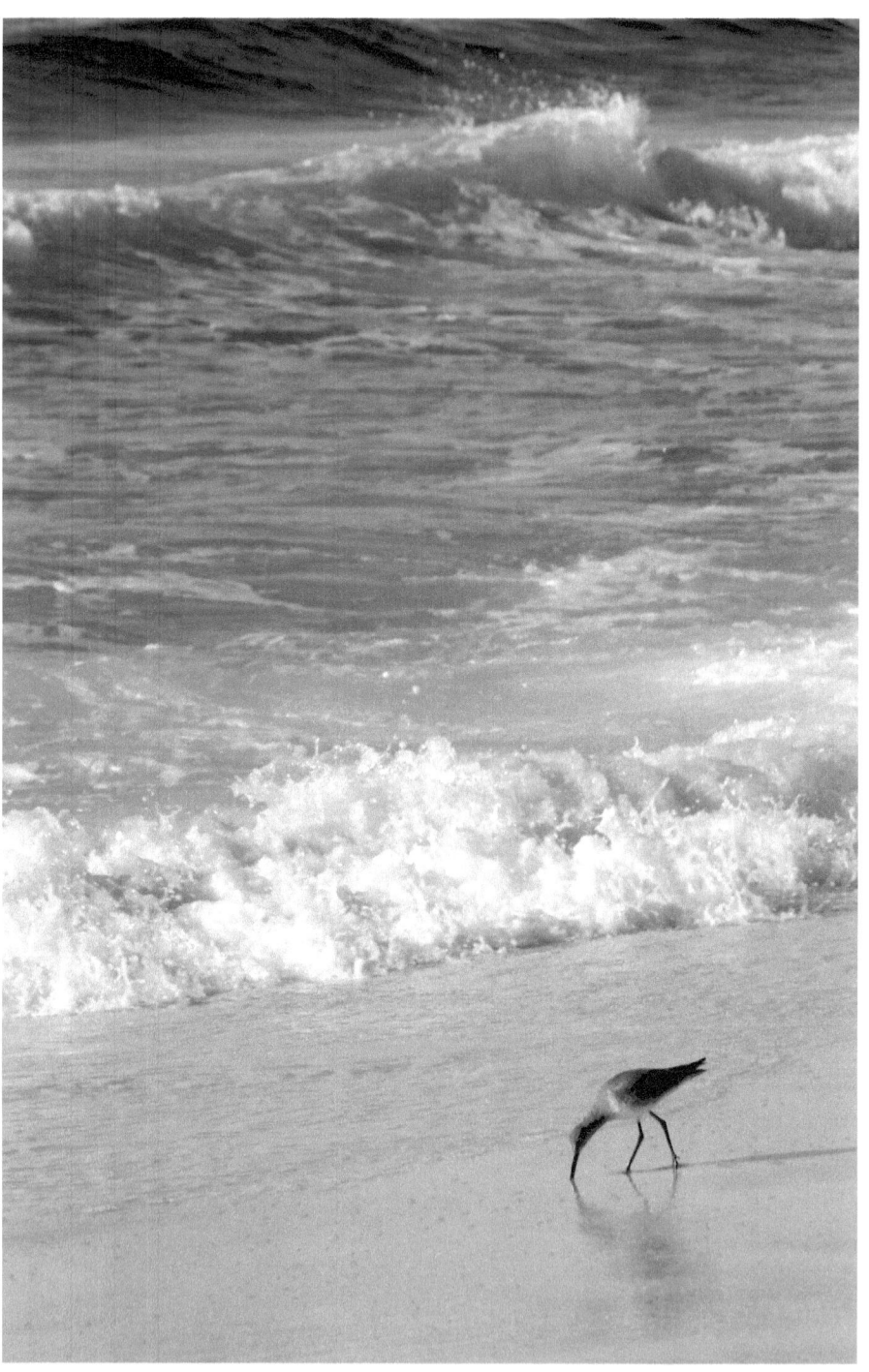

"TIME FOR DINNER"

WHAT ARE YOU SEARCHING FOR?

something, a goal to reach, or someone to meet... write it down

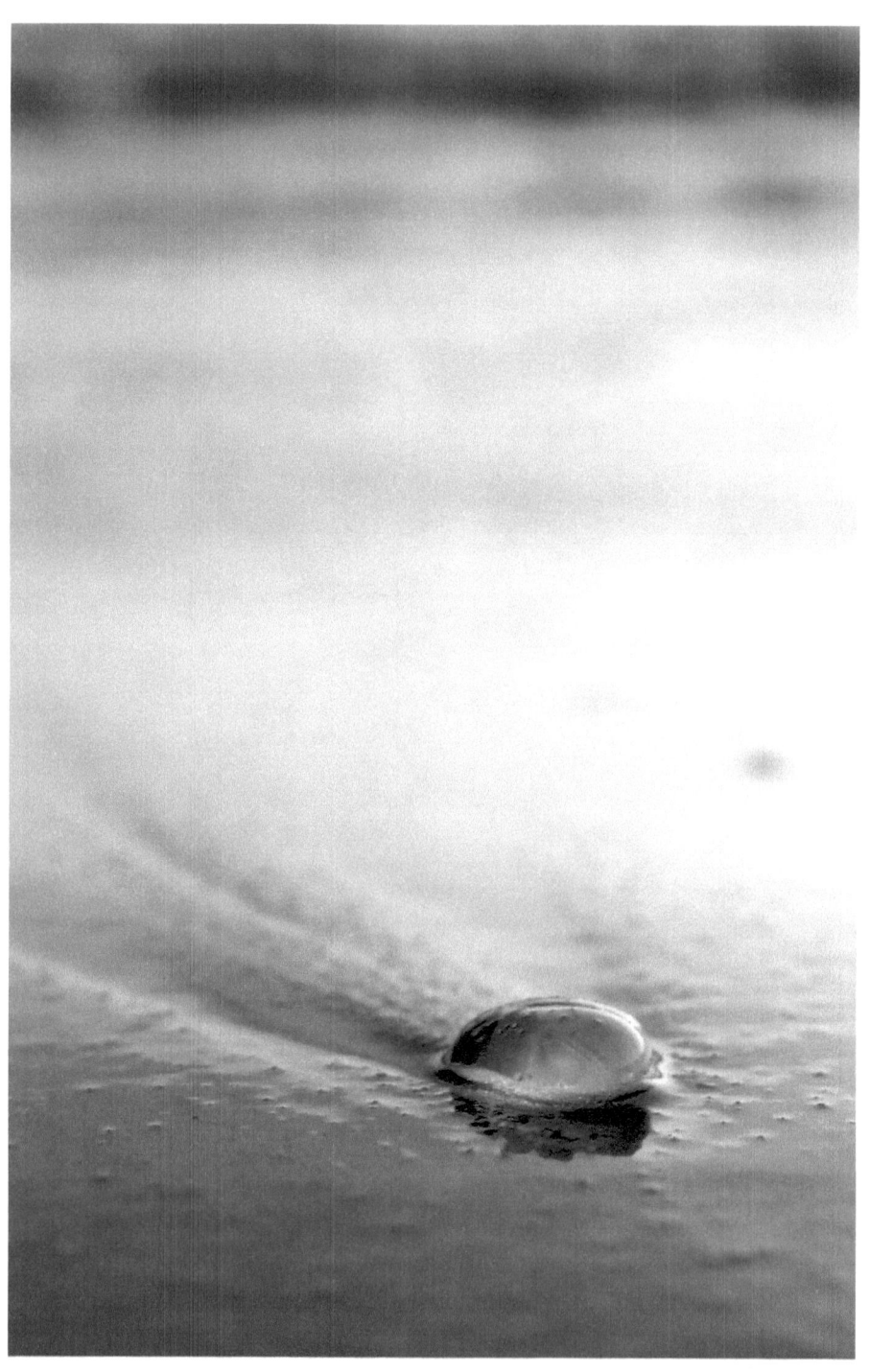

"REFLECTIONS OF A JELLYFISH"

HOW DO YOU FEEL WHEN ALONE?

write it here... the feeling and what you did to make it better

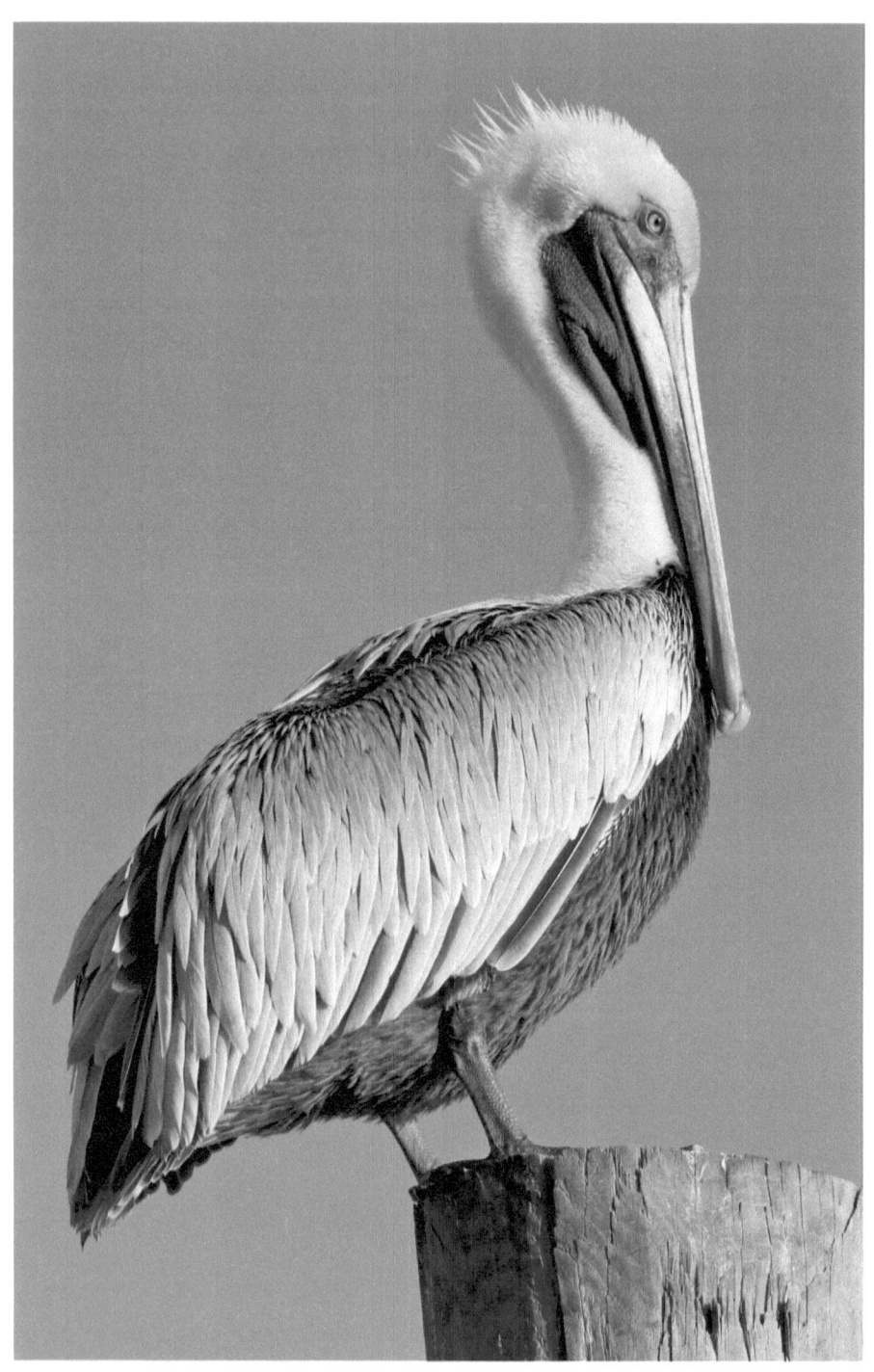

"IS THIS MY GOOD SIDE?"

WHEN DO YOU FEEL THE MOST PROUD?
think about it and write it down

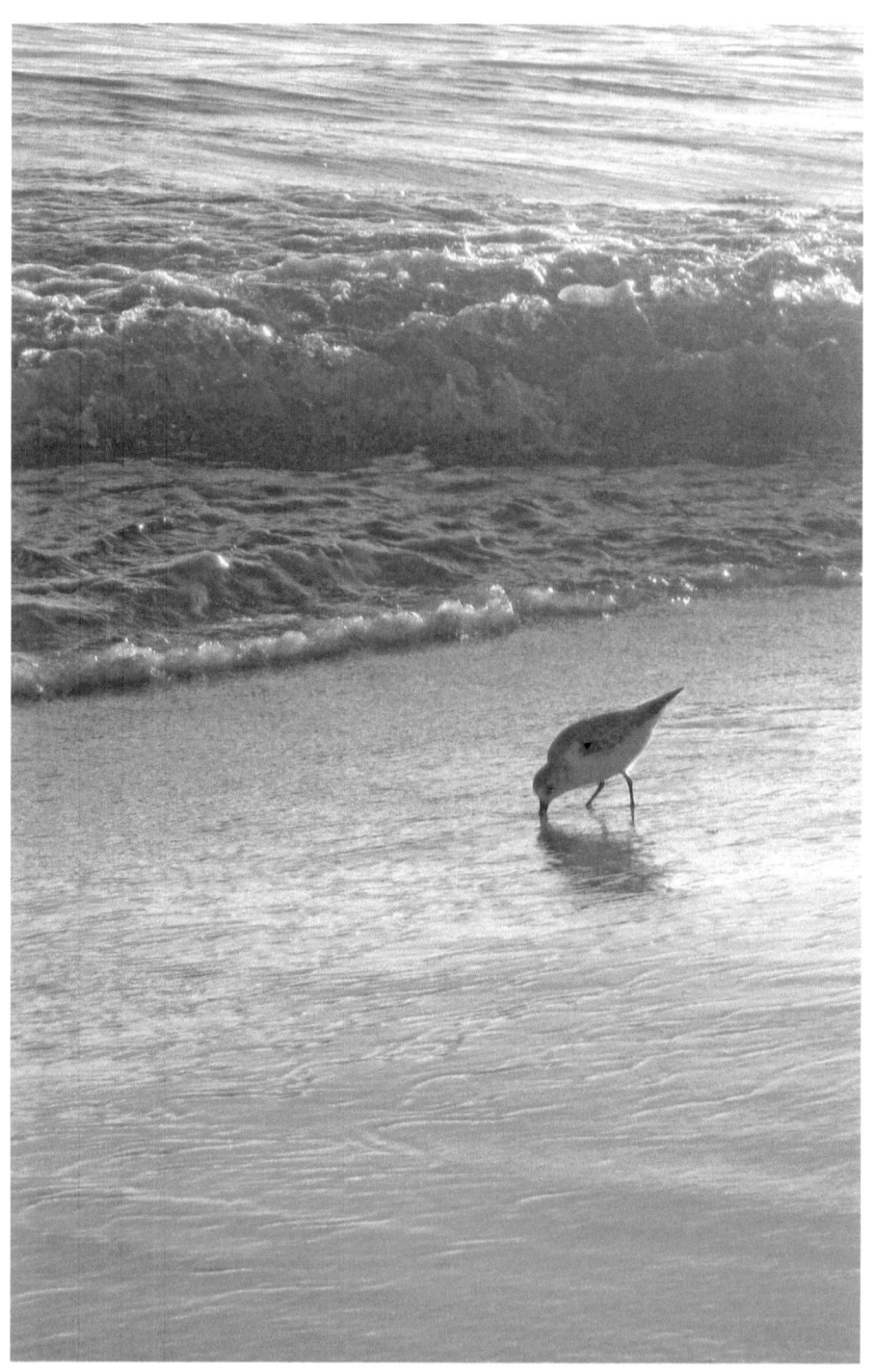

"SANDPIPER SHADOW"

WRITE THREE WORDS

what three words describe you right now? yes, it's not that easy but there
are more lines if you need to start over

_____

_____

_____

_____

_____

_____

_____

_____

_____

_____

_____

_____

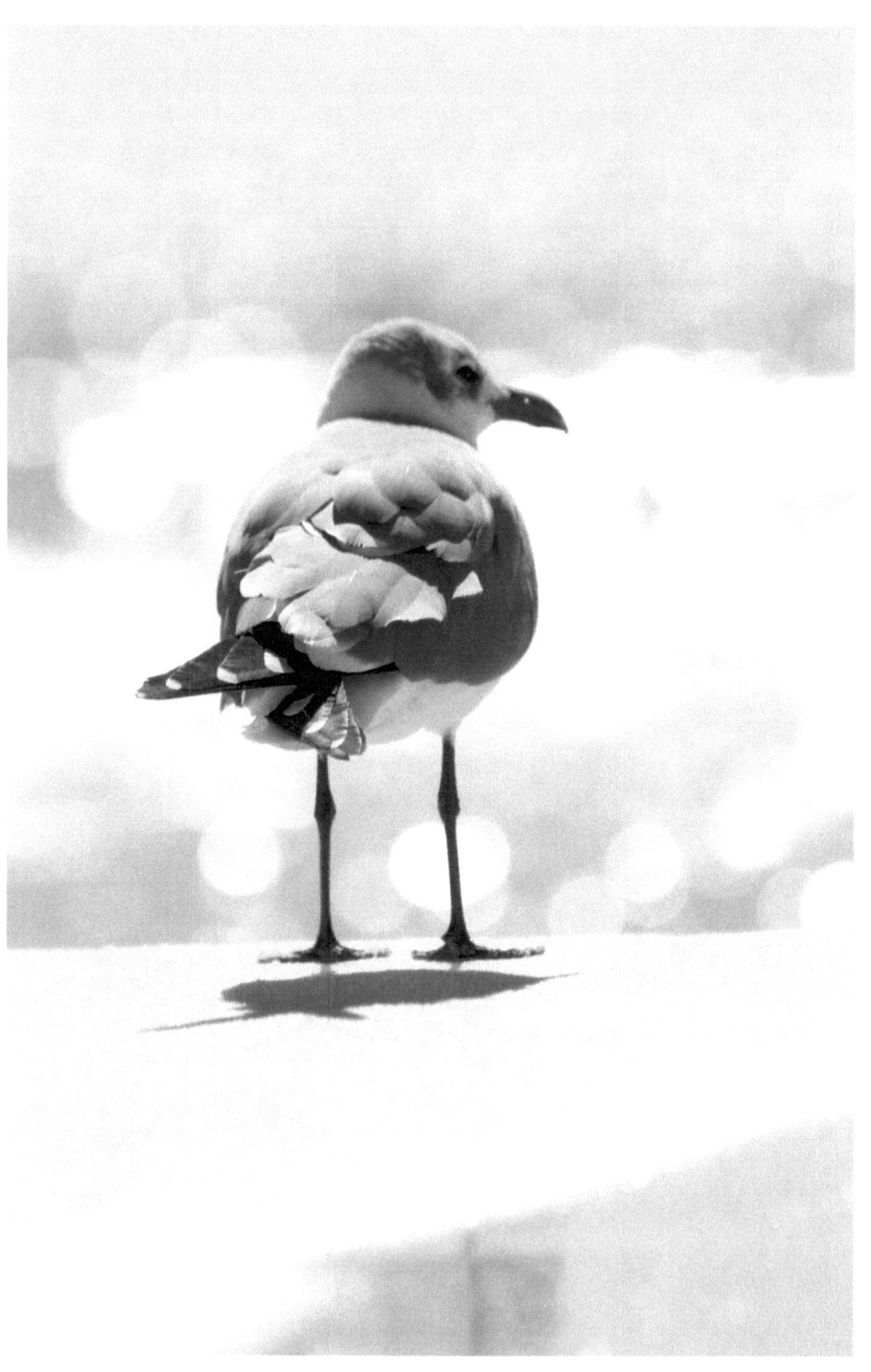

"I DON'T FEEL LIKE TALKING"

WHAT DO YOU LIKE ABOUT YOURSELF?
creativity, personality, appearance? write why you like it

draw a picture of your belly button...
you have to look at it before you start laughing

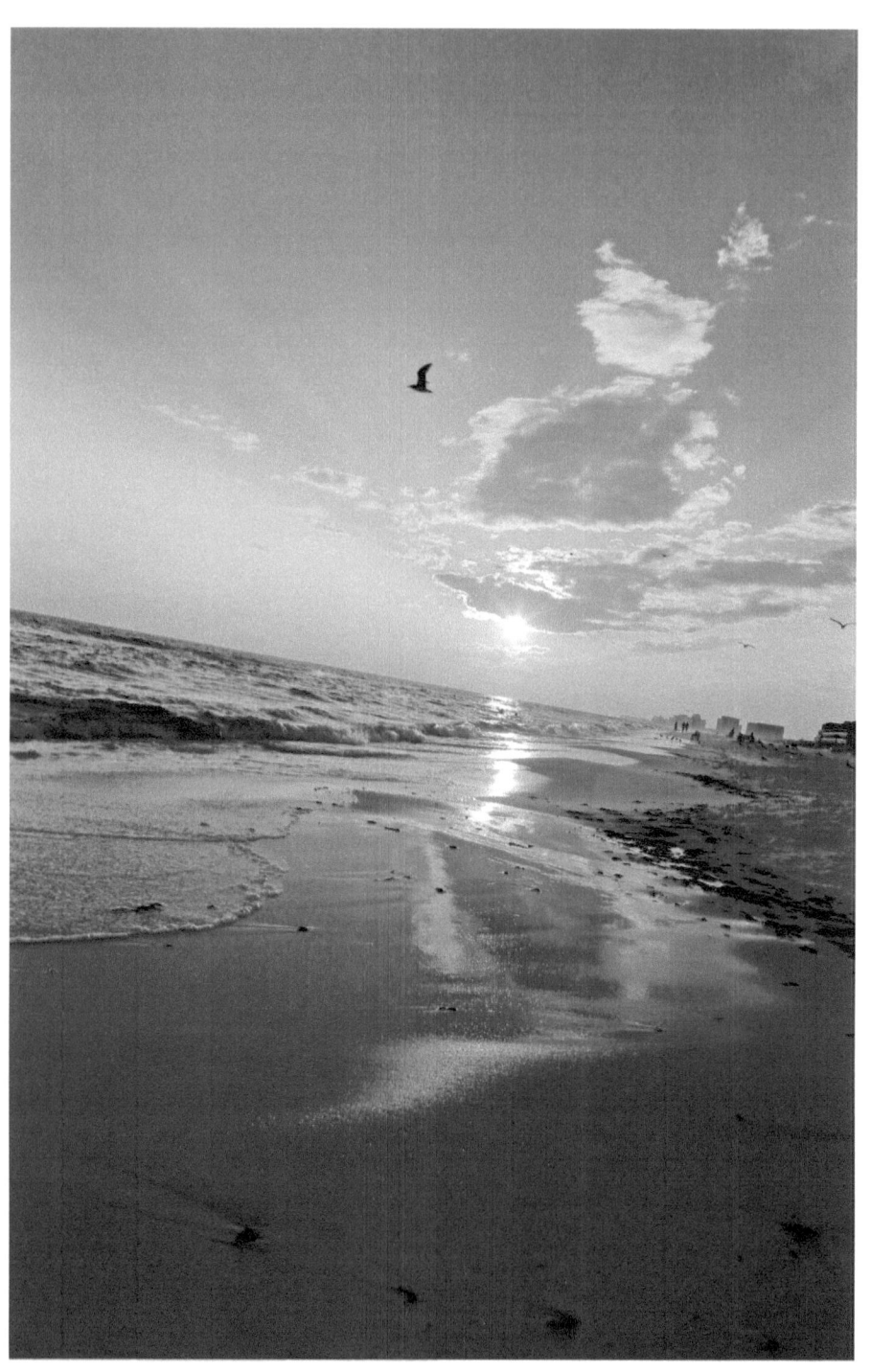

"ANOTHER WAY OF LOOKING AT IT"

WHAT HAVE YOU FOUND?

was it something strange, lost and found, collectable, or a keepsake?

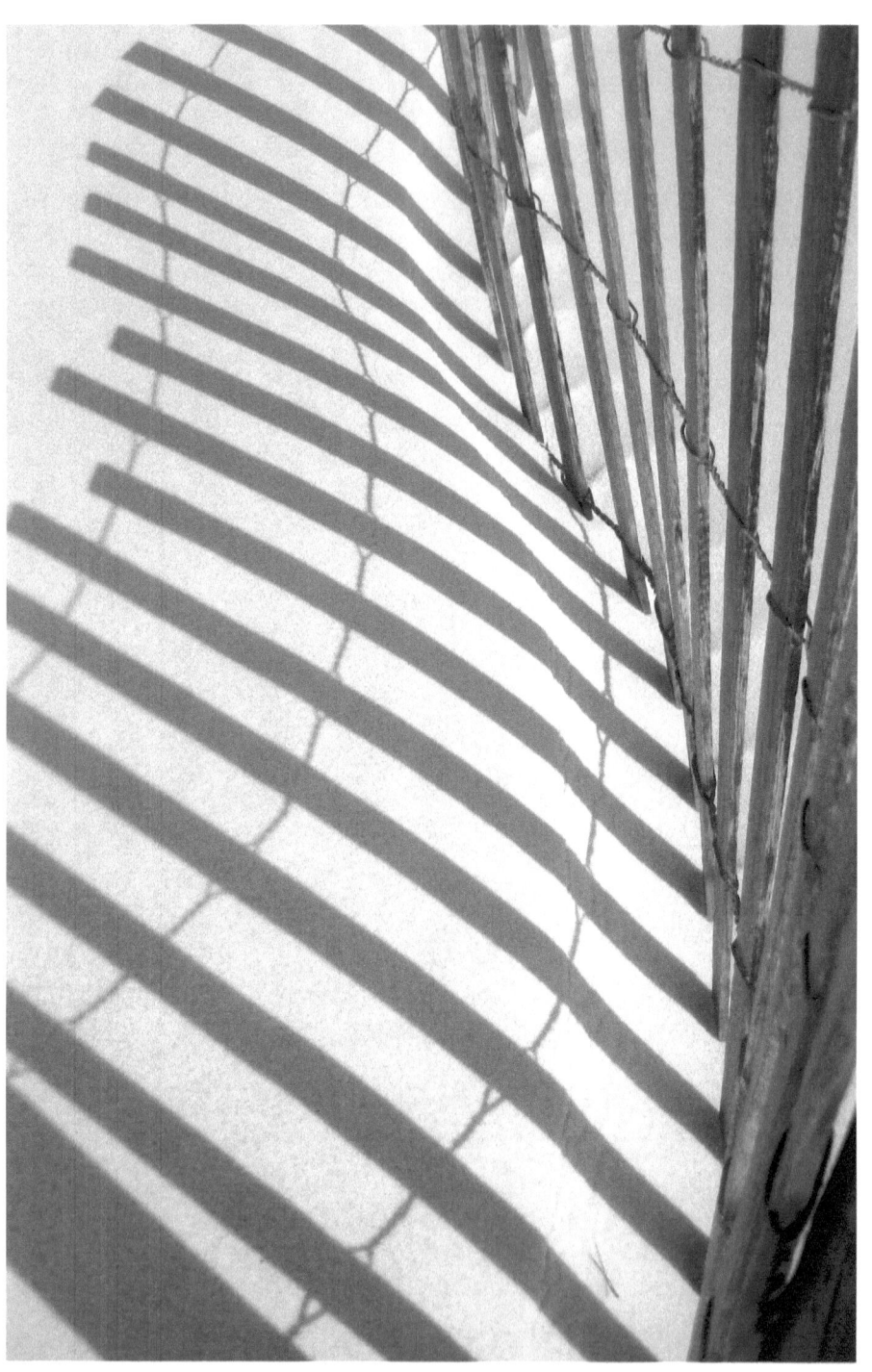

"SAND FENCE SHADOWS"

HALF FULL OR HALF EMPTY?
how do you tend to look at things and why?

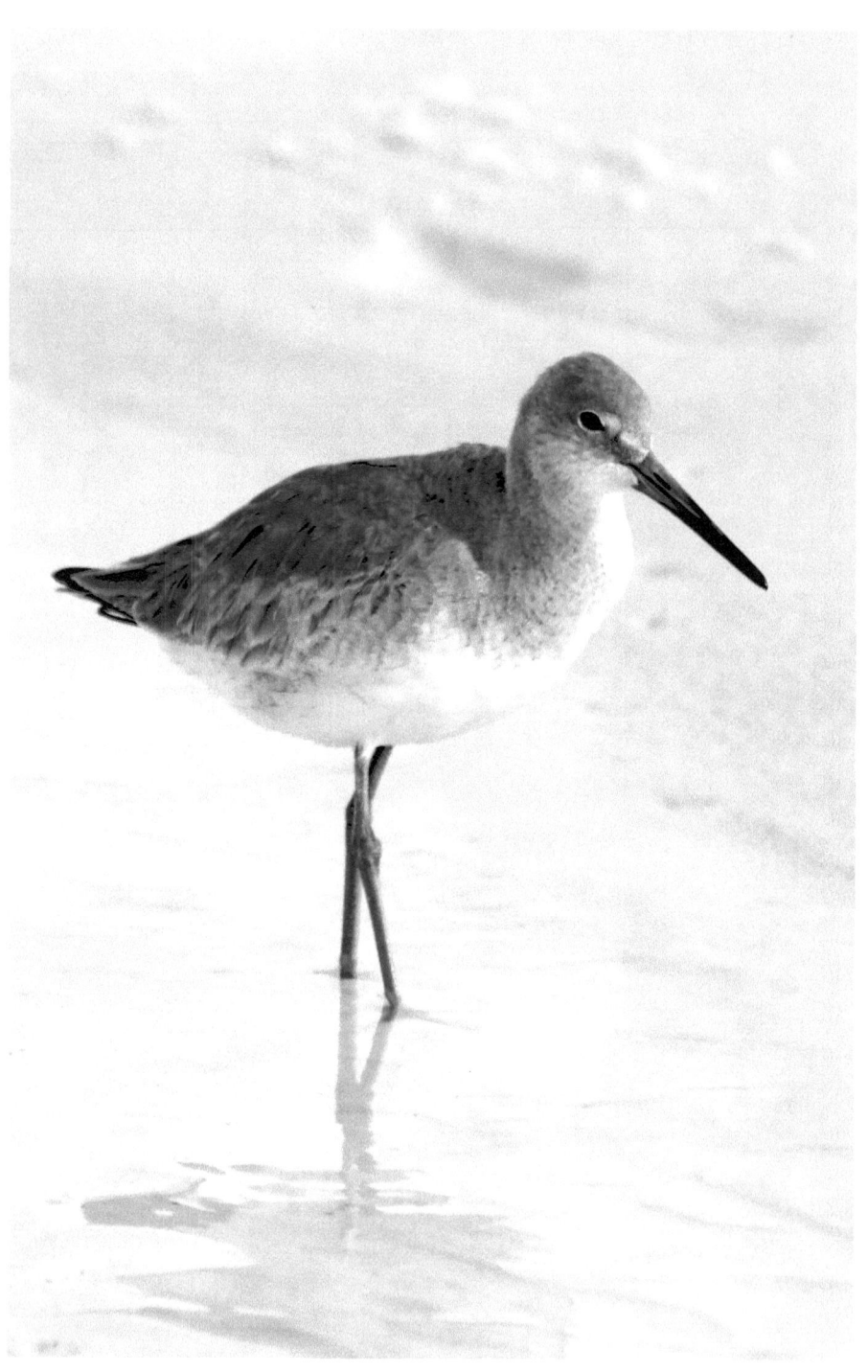

"CAN YOU SEE MY FEET?"

WOULD YOU LIKE TO BE FAMOUS?

why or why not? what would you be famous for?

NORTHWEST FLORIDA... another day in Destin

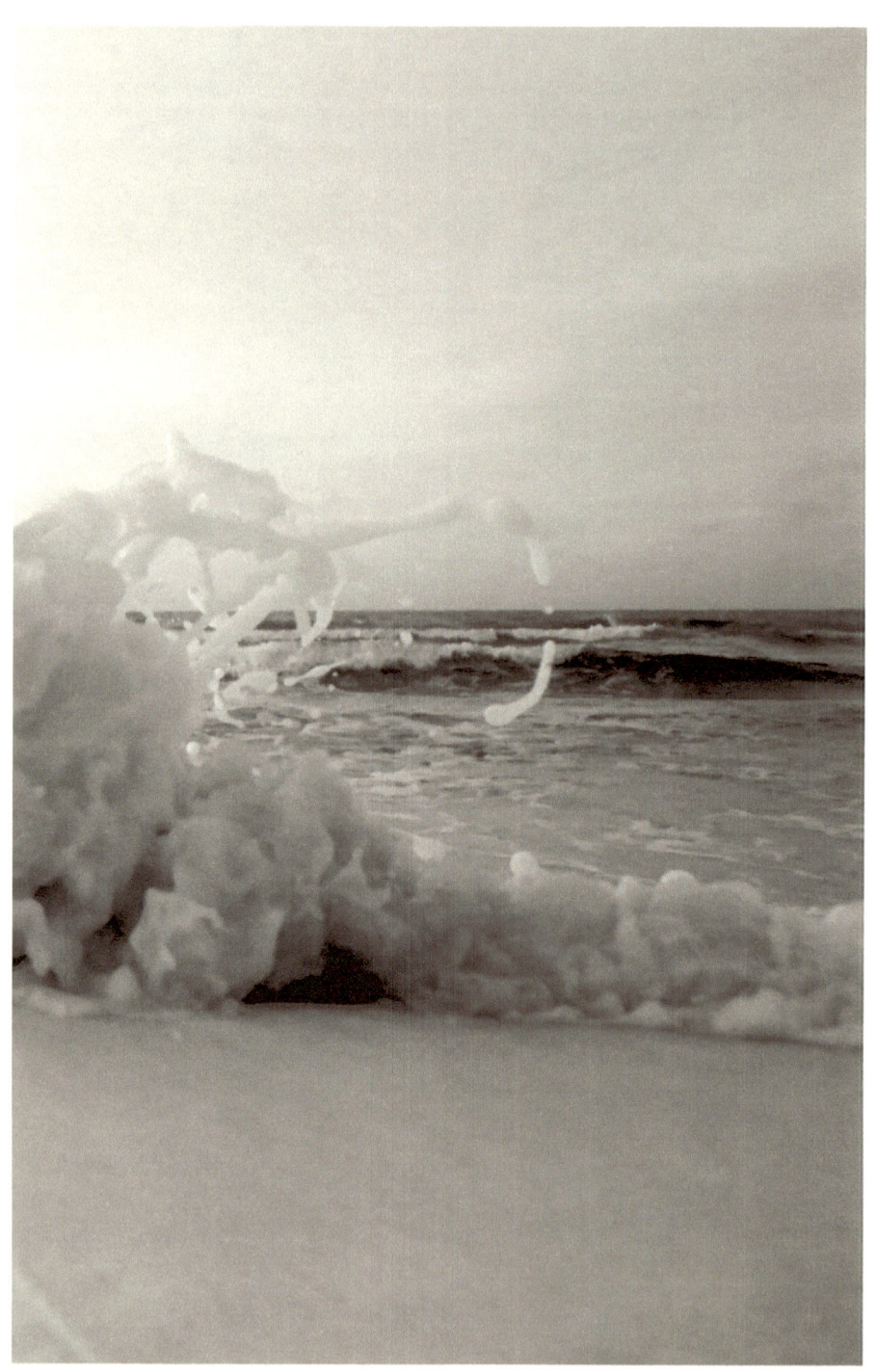

"WOAH, THIS JUST HAPPENED"

WHAT MAKES A FRIEND IMPORTANT?
loyalty, generosity, honesty? write down why

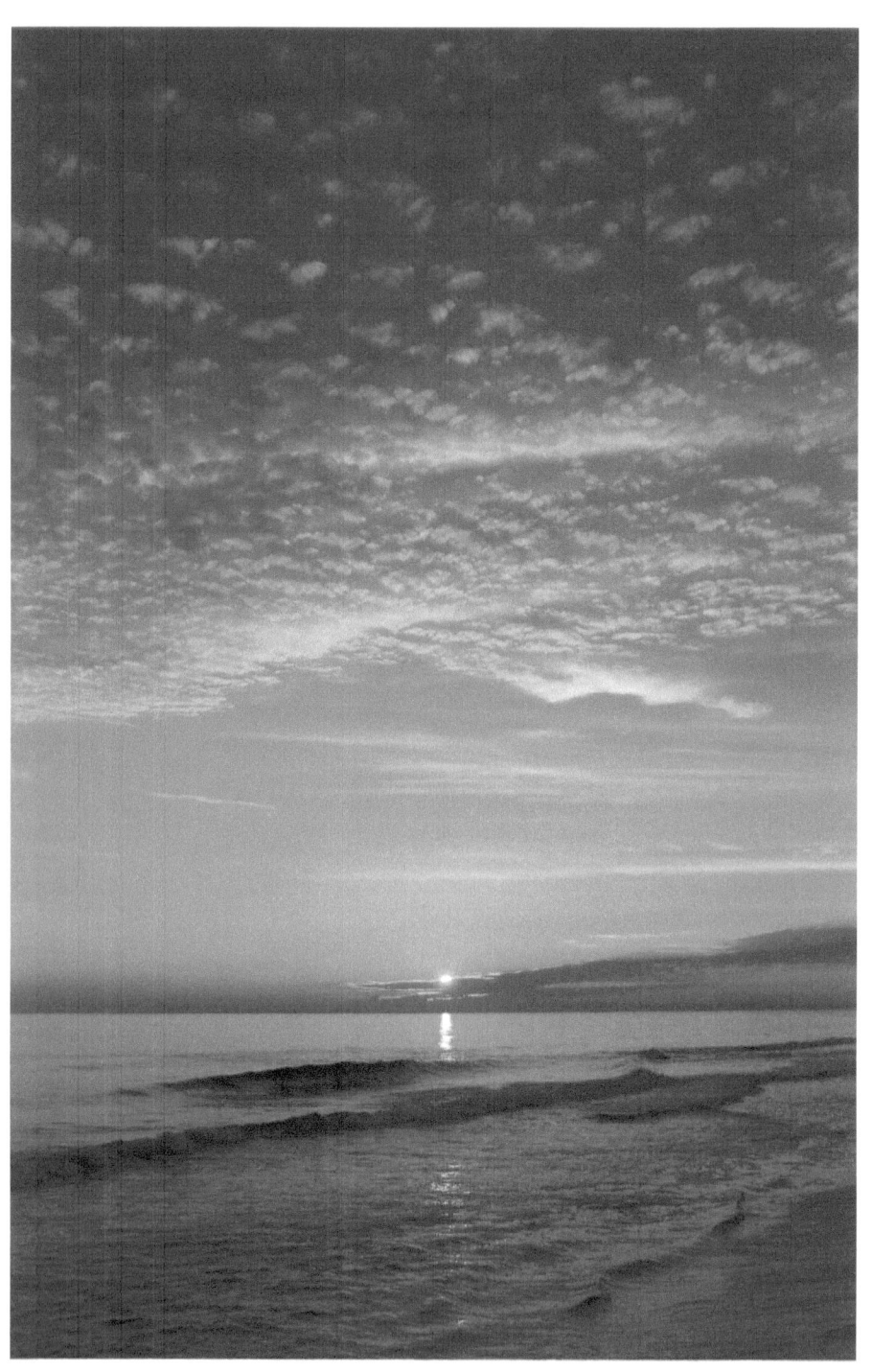

"IMAGINE THOSE CLOUDS ARE PINK"

UNLIMITED ACCESS TO MONEY

how would you spend it? write down how and why

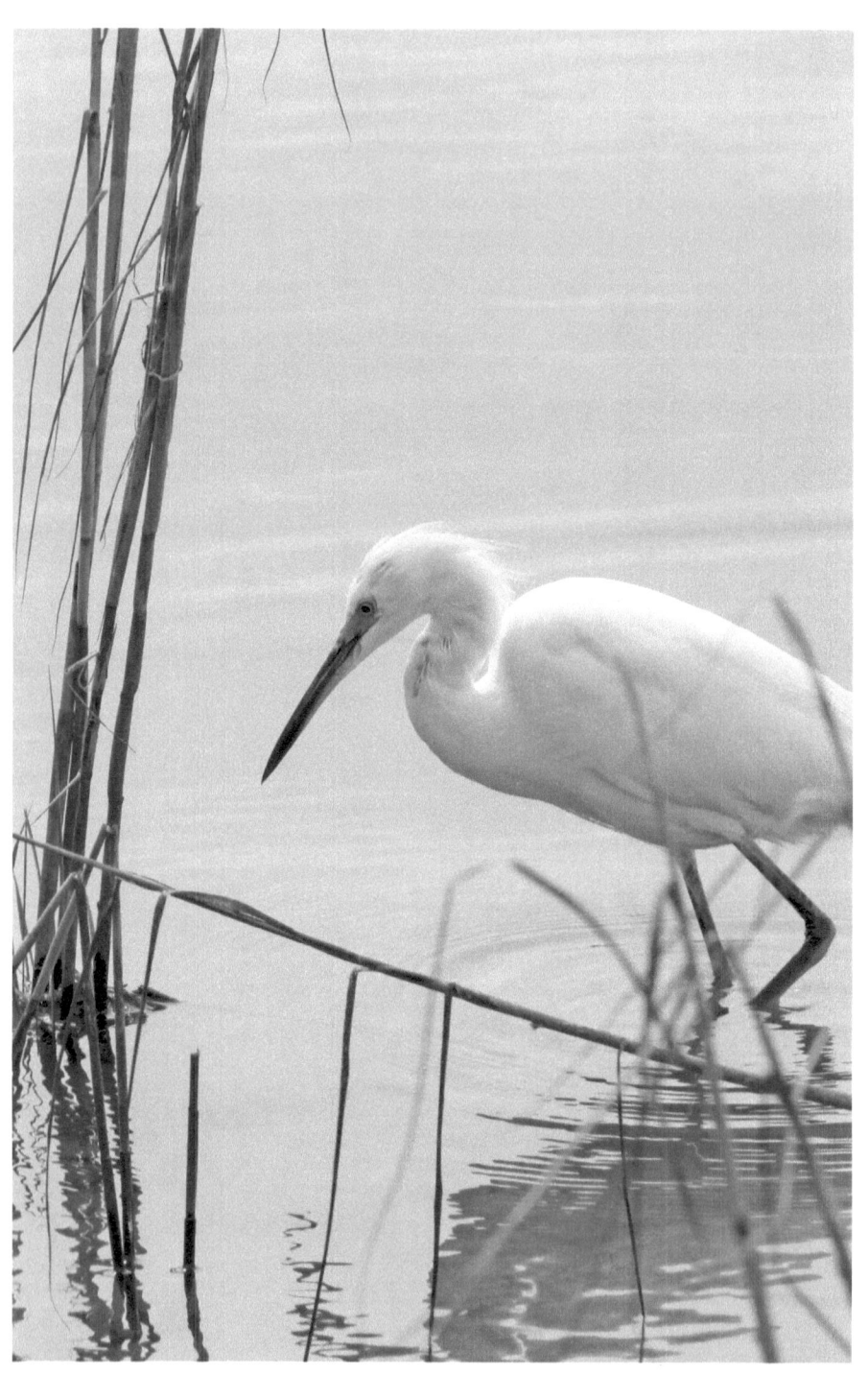

"HUNTING BY THE BAY"

WHAT DO YOU TEACH OTHERS?

tell me the last thing you taught someone. how did it make you feel to share your knowledge?

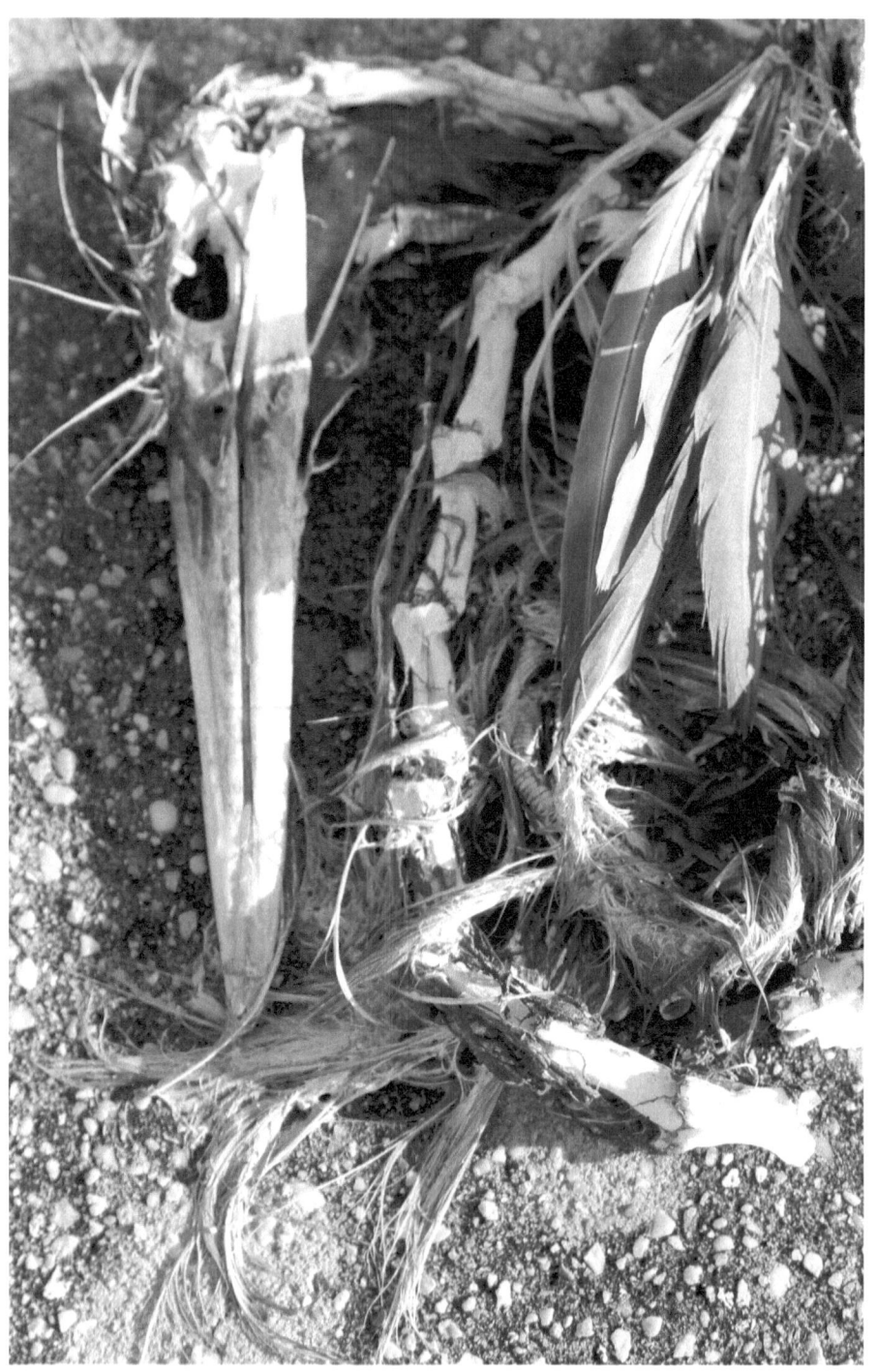

"WE DON'T LAST FOREVER"

THE GREAT BLUE HERON'S LAST FLIGHT

write a story about what it may have been

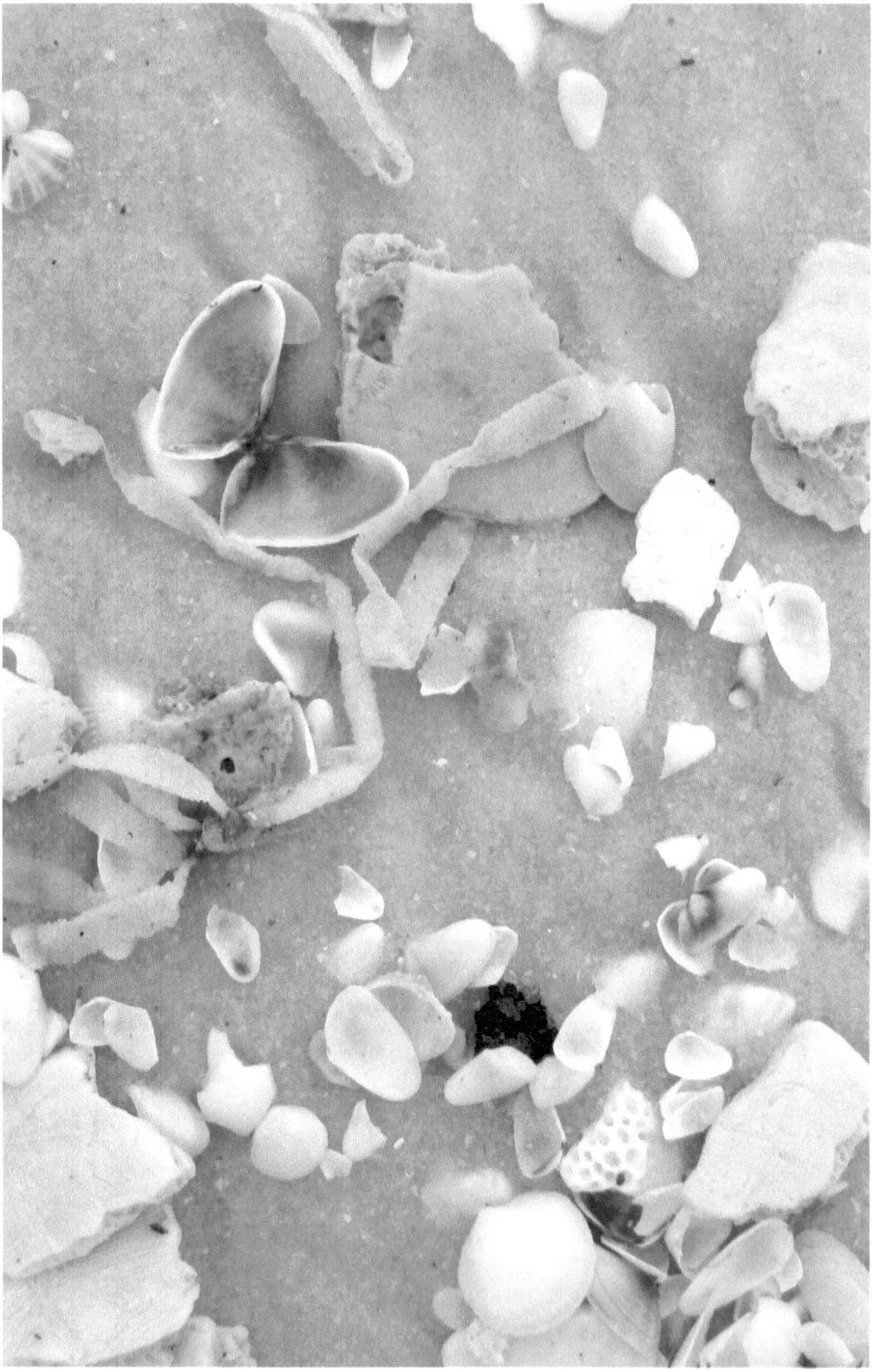

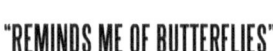

"REMINDS ME OF BUTTERFLIES"

DRAW SOME SEA SHELLS YOU LIKE
the sand is easy to draw and the shells are fun to color

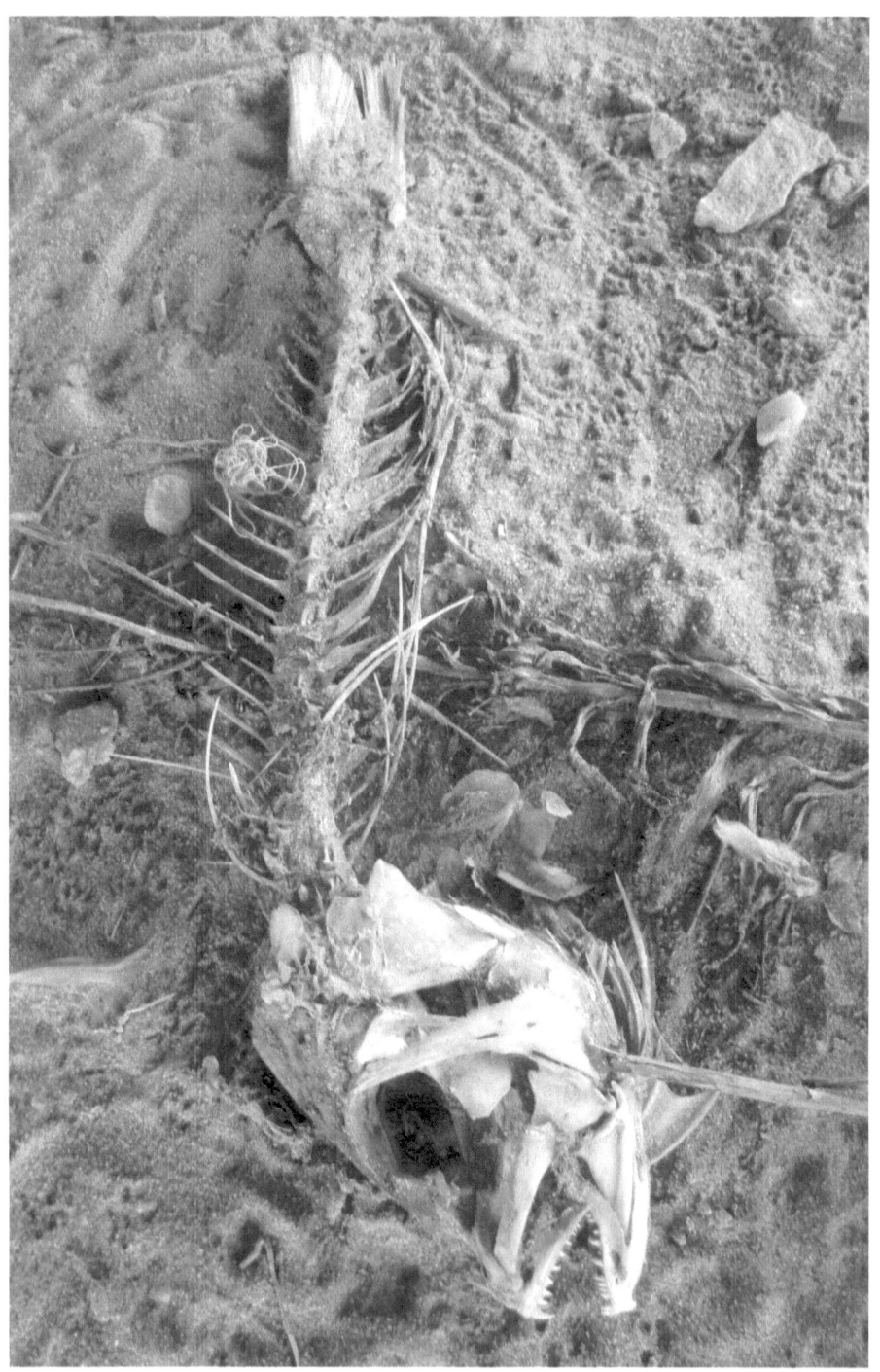

"HE WAS SOMEONE'S MEAL"

WHAT DID YOU EAT WHILE HERE?

seafood, steak, or fast food? write where you went. would you eat there again? did you leave a tip? any comments? spill it out...

NORTHWEST FLORIDA... another day in Destin

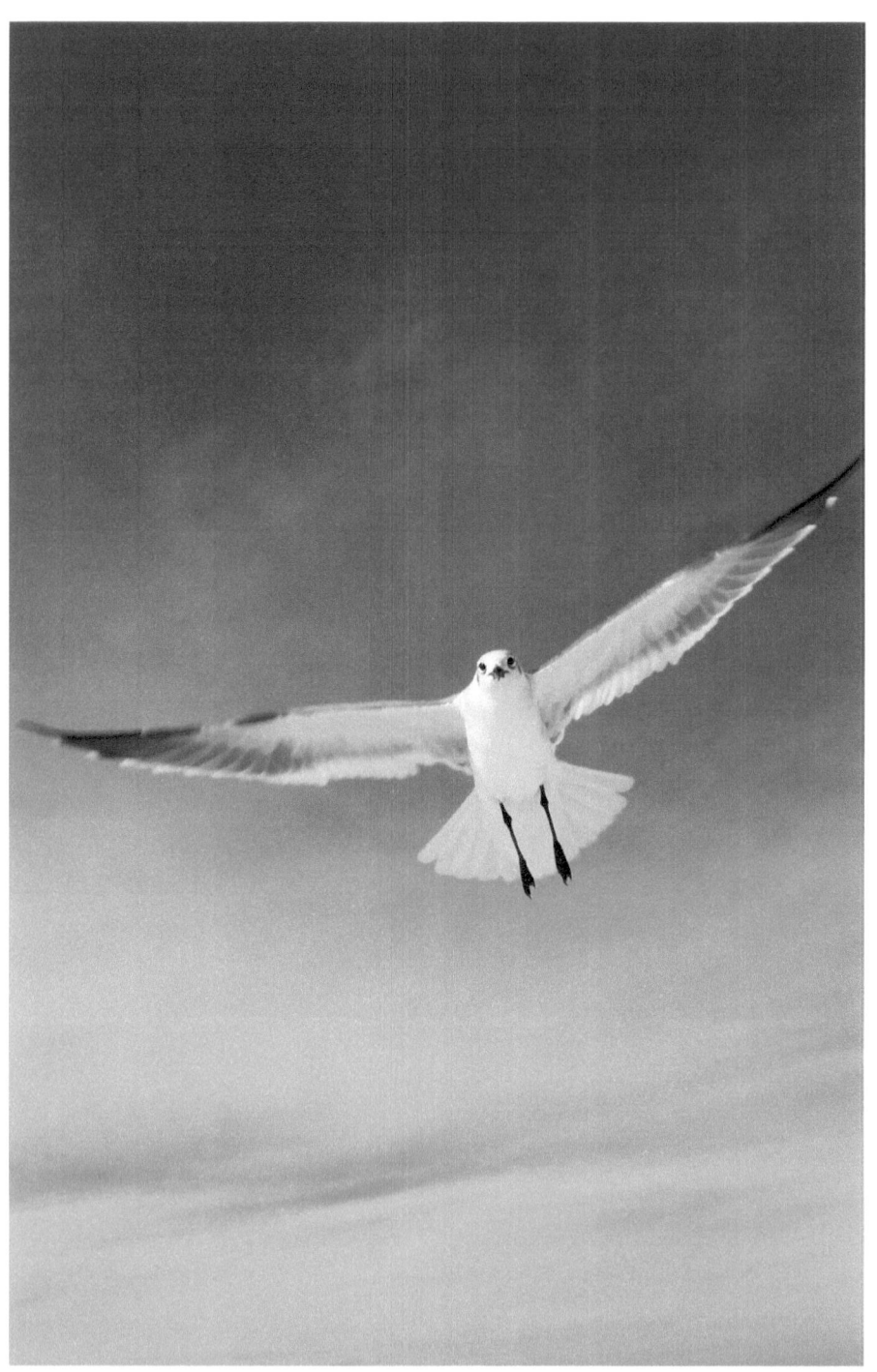

"IT CAME FROM ABOVE"

DESCRIBE YOUR LIFE
exciting, glamorous, organized, boring, dull? why?

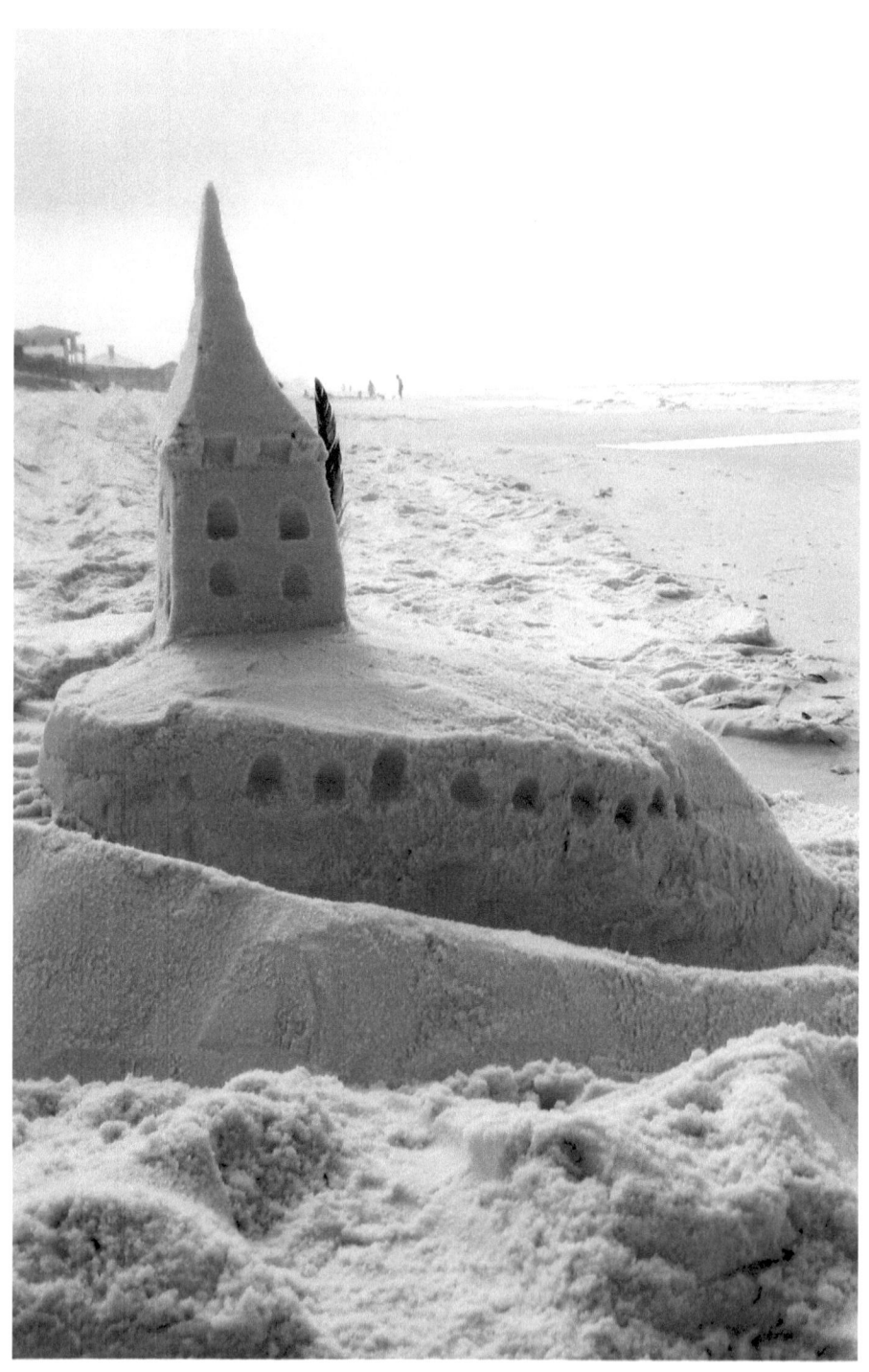

"LET'S BUILD IT TOGETHER"

DRAW YOUR OWN SANDCASTLE
use dots, lines, or whatever you feel like using

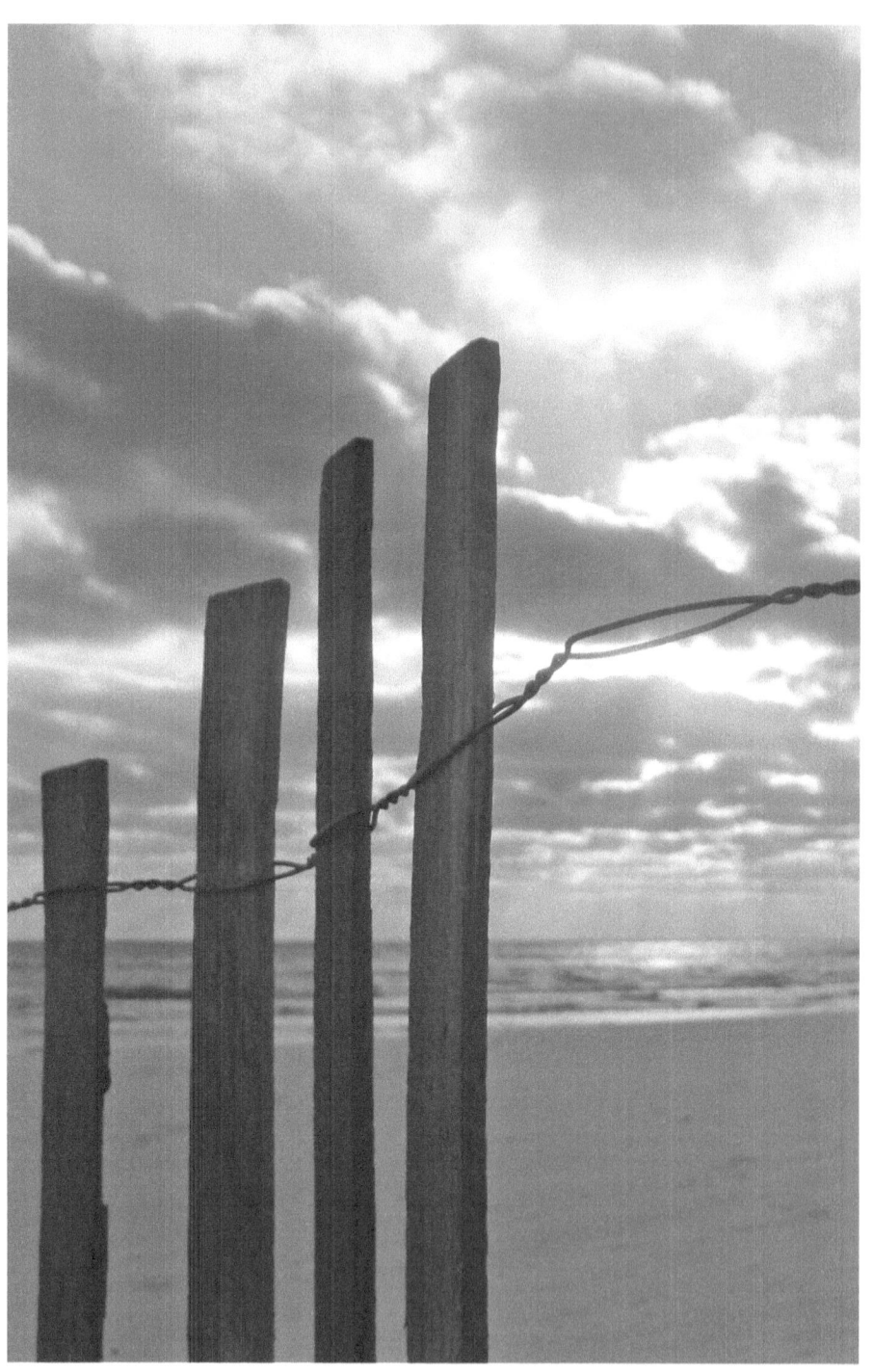

"PROTECT THE DUNES"

WHAT WOULD YOU GET RID OF?
if you could eliminate one thing in the world, what would it be and why?

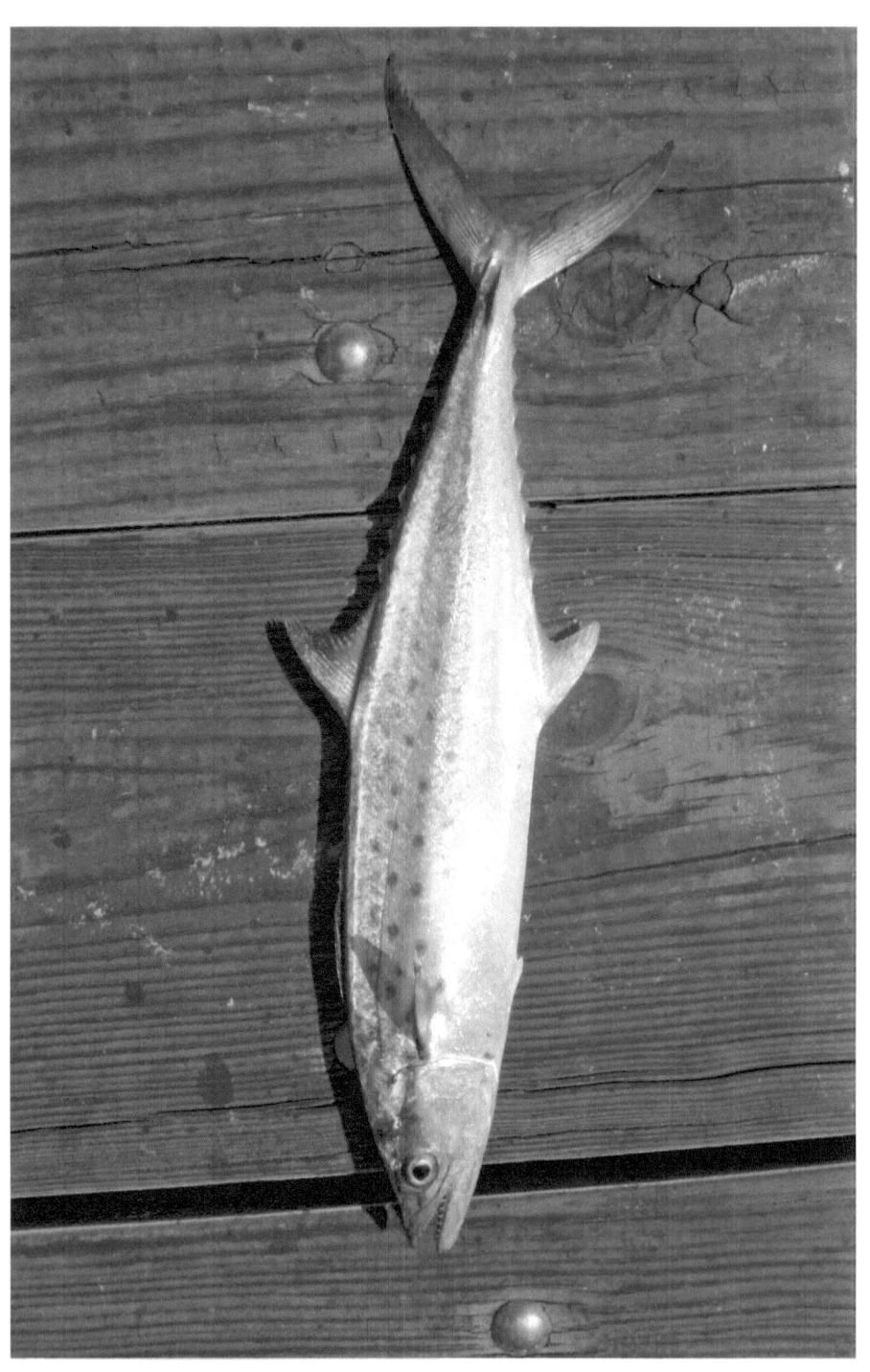

"I SPEAK A LITTLE SPANISH MACKEREL"

WHO TAUGHT YOU TO FISH?

love it or hate it all of us have tried fishing... write about it. what bait did you use? did you catch anything or just have a good time with others?

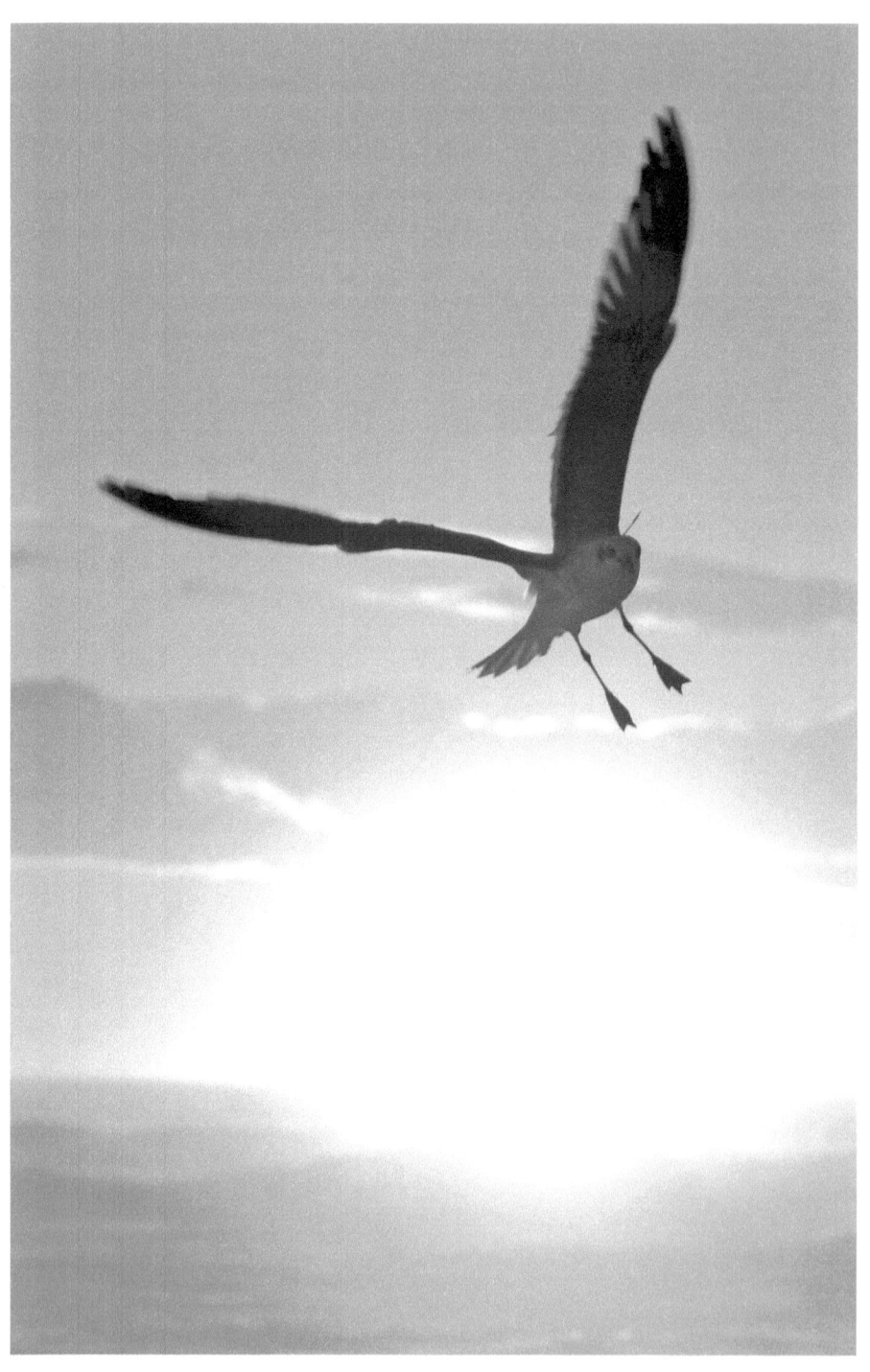

"COMING HOME"

WHERE DO YOU GO FROM HERE?

what are you looking forward to? write down some goals or dreams here

_____

_____

_____

_____

_____

_____

_____

_____

_____

_____

_____

_____

_____

_____

_____

_____

_____

_____

_____

_____

_____

_____

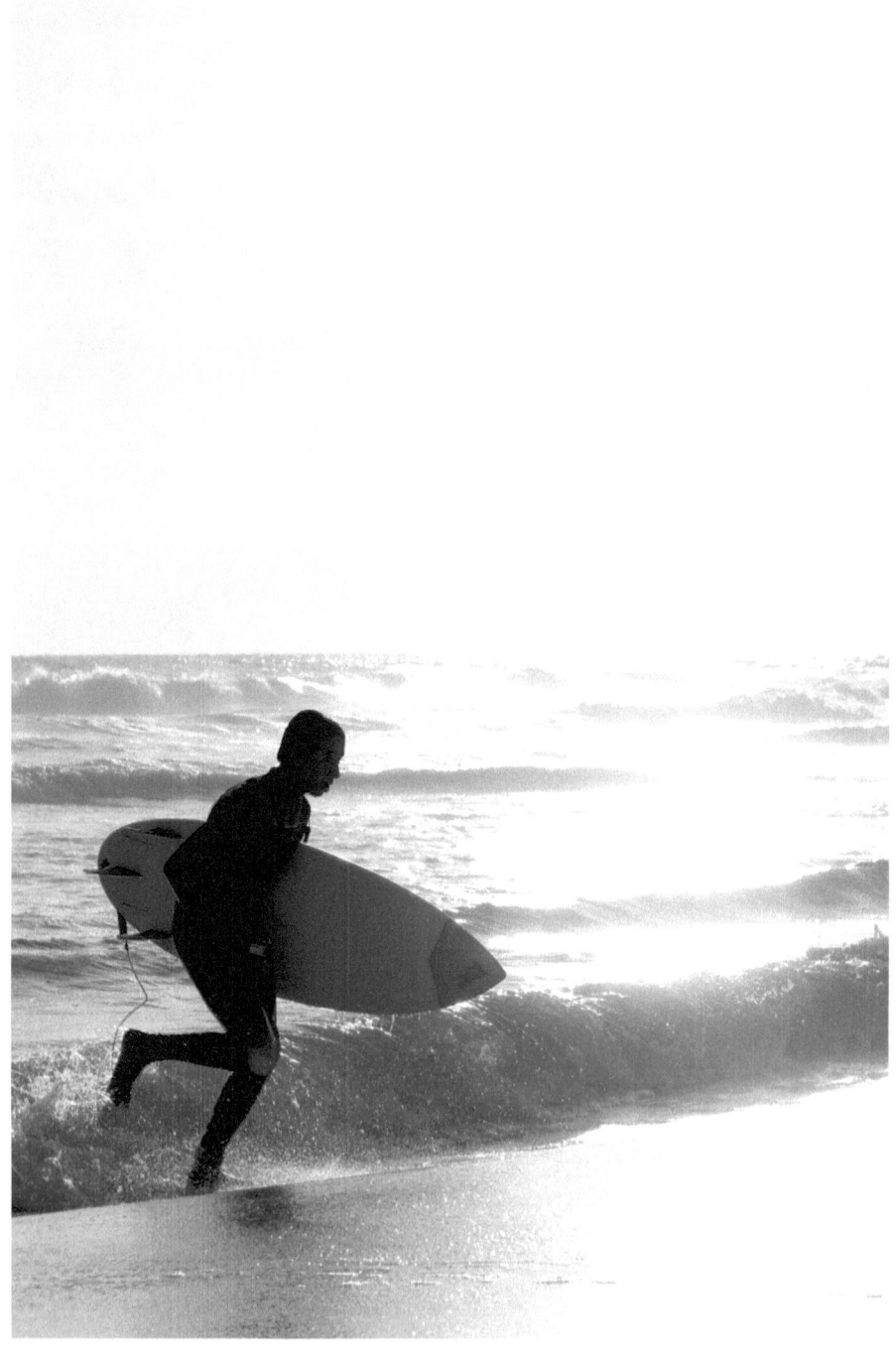

"SHORTBOARD SURFER"

WHAT SPORTS DO YOU LIKE AND WHY?
everyone needs to play even if it's not a sport... write down your favorites

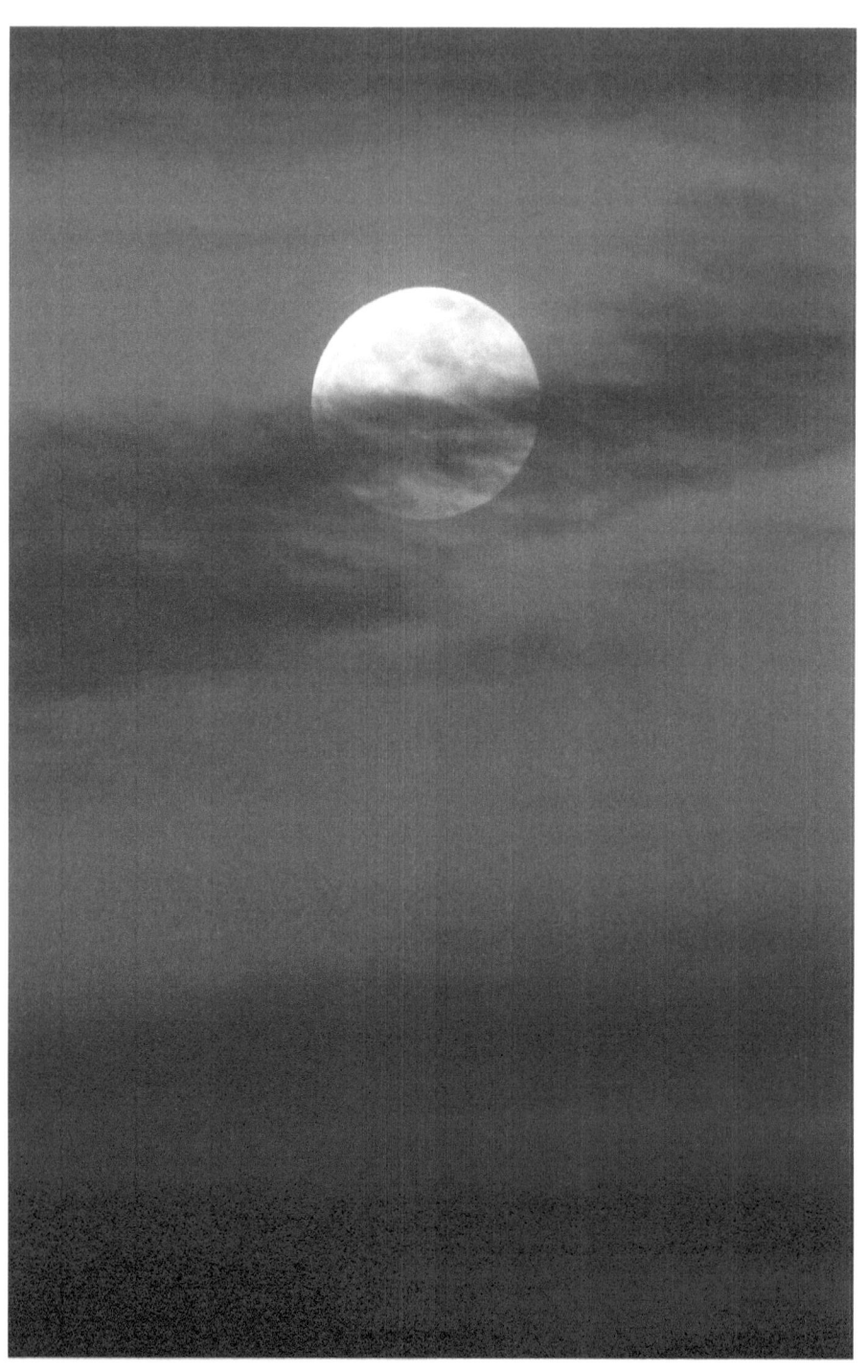

"ANOTHER FULL MOON"

WHAT DO YOU THINK ABOUT...

when you look up in the sky and see things you can't reach?

_____

_____

_____

_____

_____

_____

_____

_____

_____

_____

_____

_____

_____

_____

_____

_____

_____

_____

_____

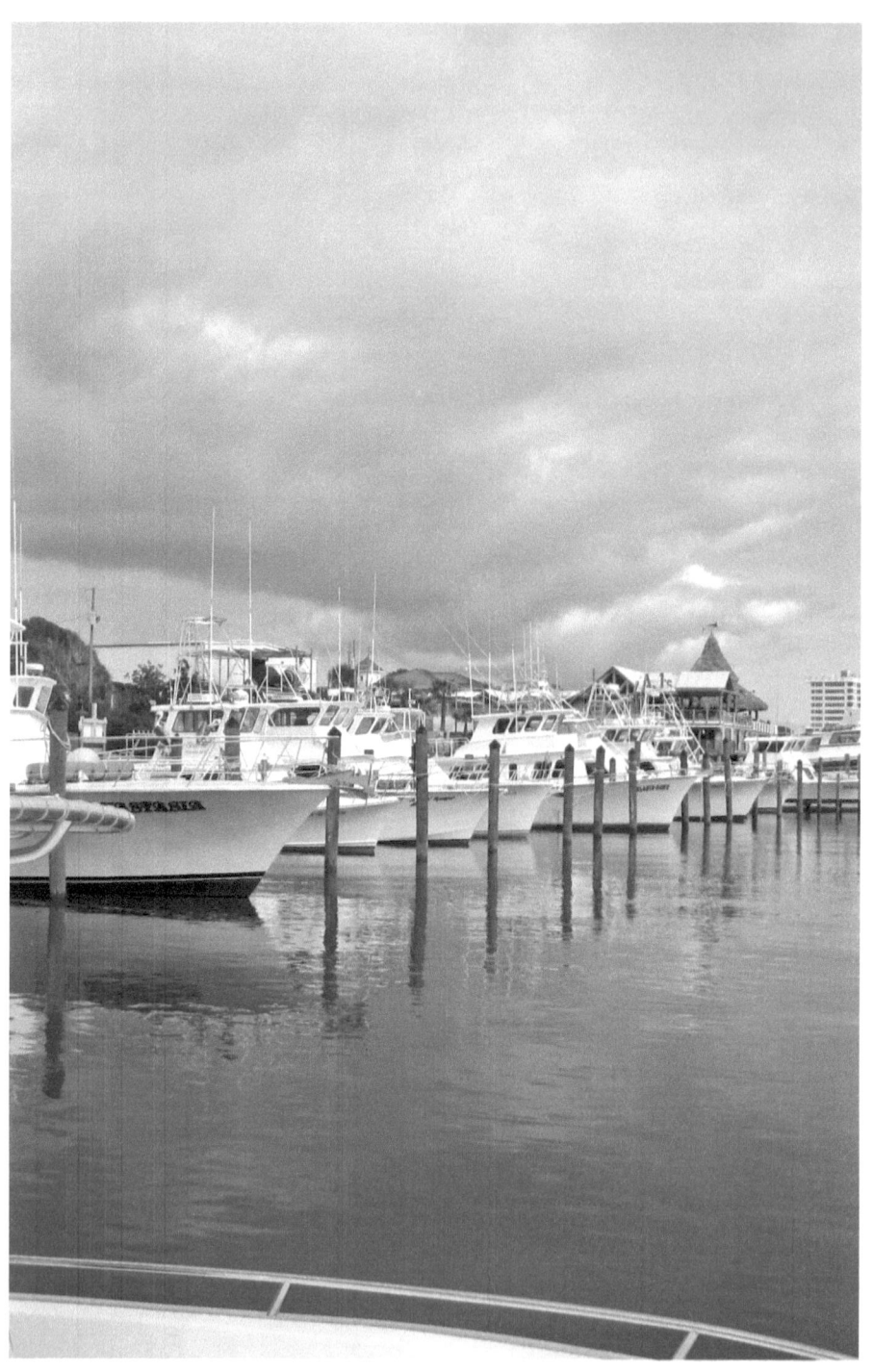

"BEFORE THE STORM"

WHAT DOES THE HARBOR SMELL LIKE?

close your eyes and see if you can smell it

_____

_____

_____

_____

_____

_____

_____

_____

_____

_____

_____

_____

_____

_____

_____

_____

_____

_____

_____

_____

_____

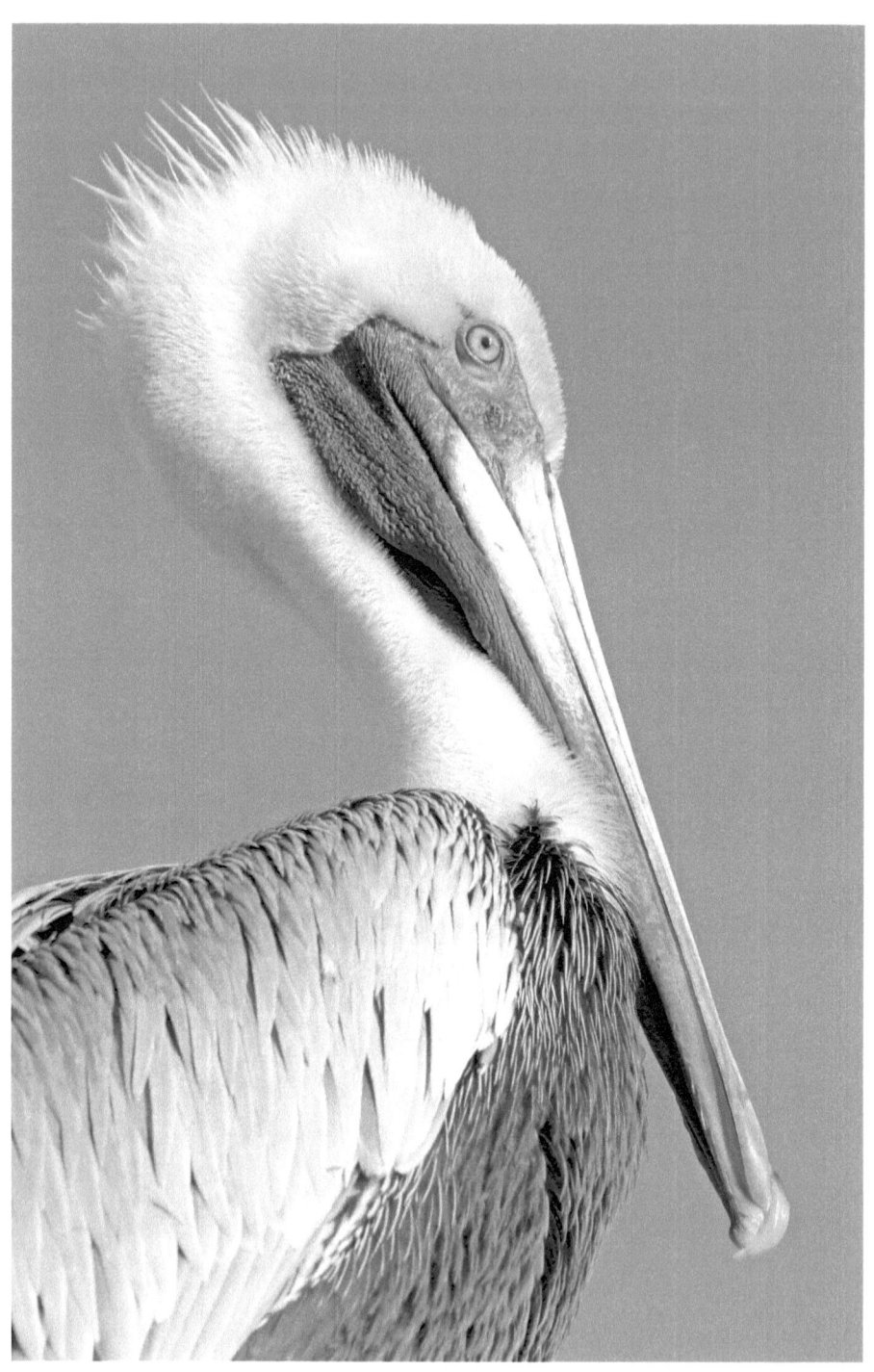

"I AM A PELICAN"

WHY DOES PREJUDICE EXIST?
write what you think and how it has affected you

_____

_____

_____

_____

_____

_____

_____

_____

_____

_____

_____

_____

_____

_____

_____

_____

_____

_____

_____

_____

_____

_____

_____

_____

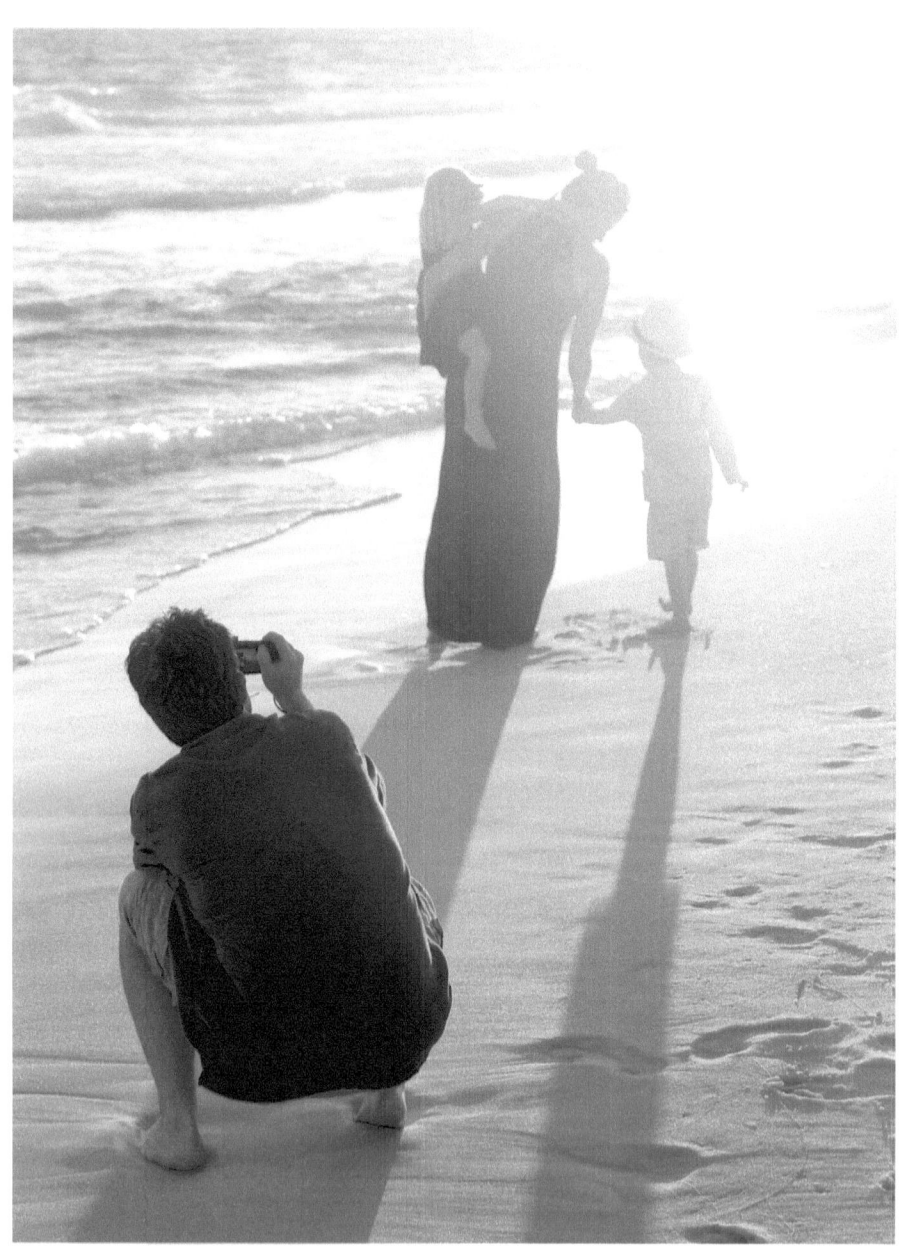

"MAKING MEMORIES"

MEMORABLE CHILDHOOD LESSON
what did you learn from it?

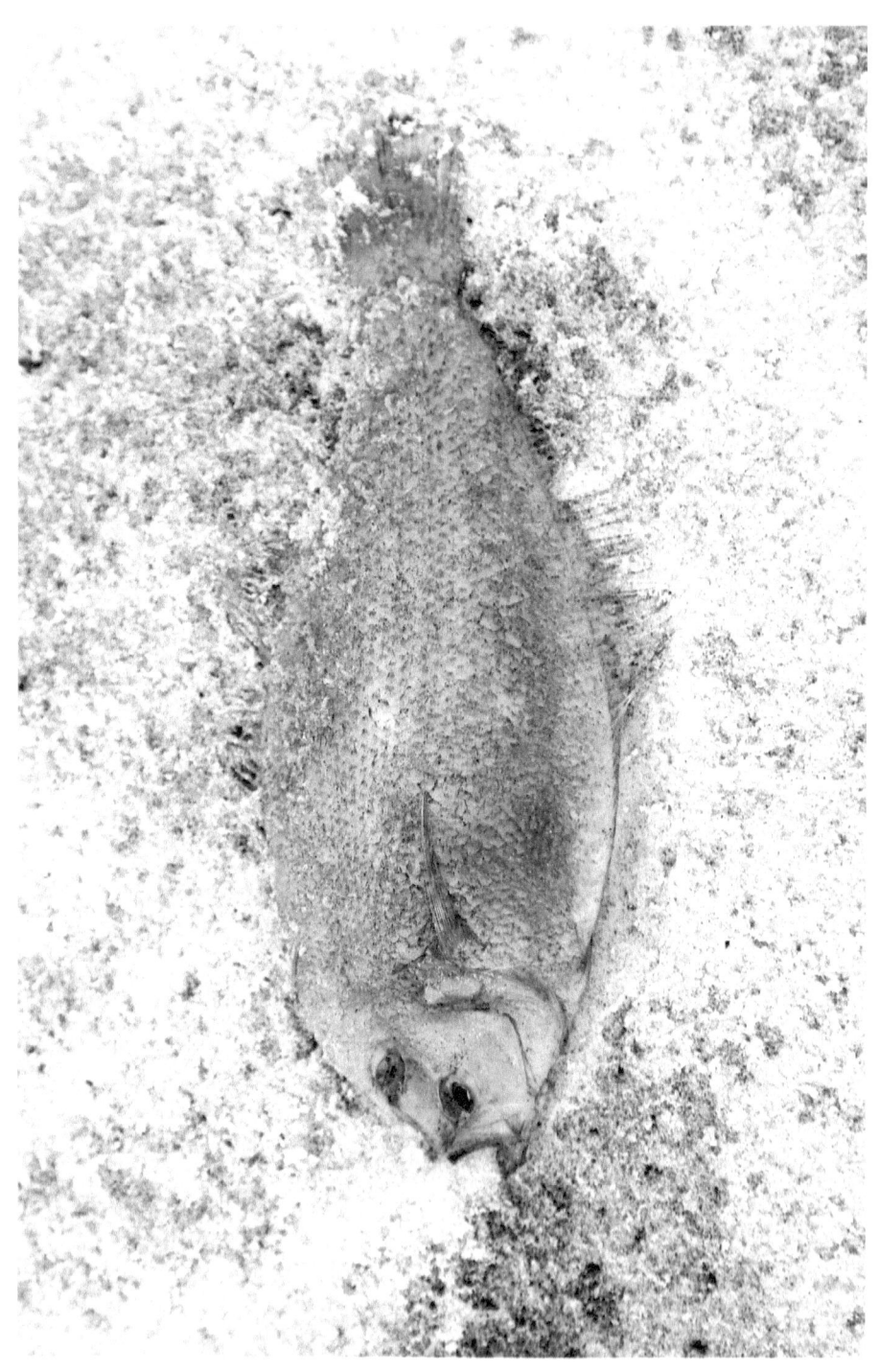

"THE RED TIDE IS NOT A GOOD THING"

REMEMBER ME?

how do you want to be remembered when you're gone?

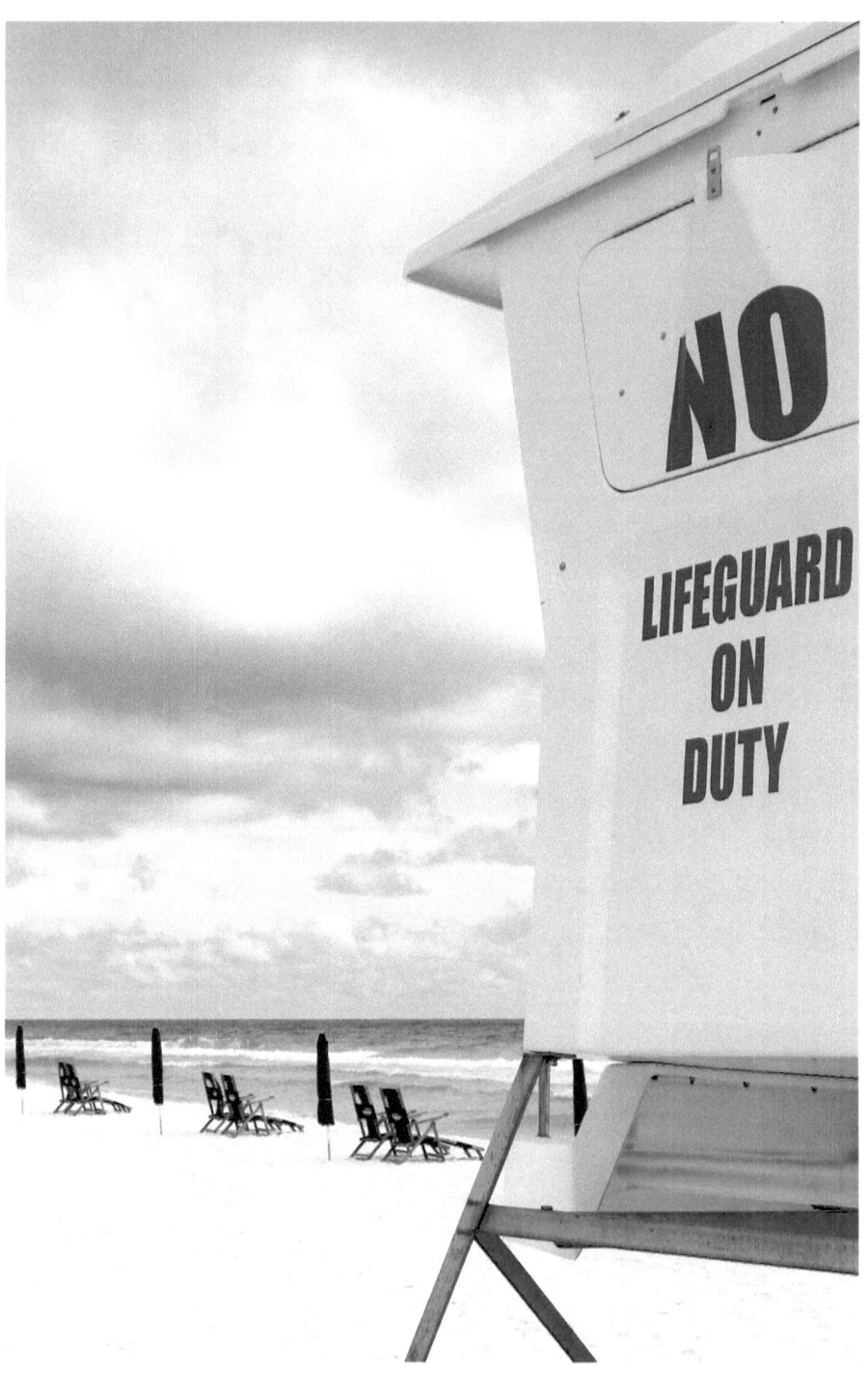

"OFF SEASON"

WHAT MAKES YOU FEEL SECURE?

write what or who makes you feel safe and out of harms way

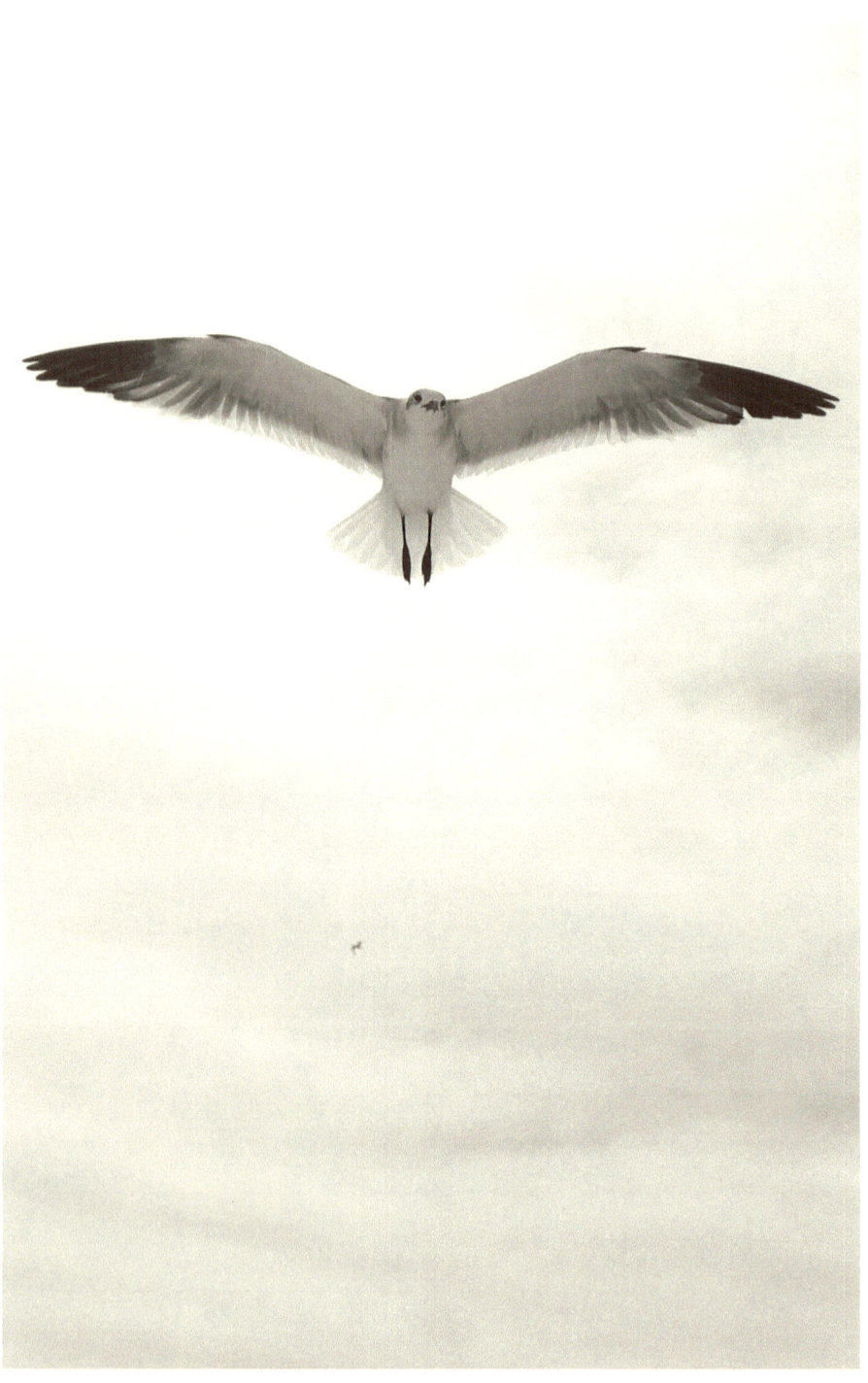

"I SEE POTATO CHIPS"

HOW DO YOU FEEL?

in one word per line (or more words if you need to vent)
write how you feel when people look down on you

NORTHWEST FLORIDA... another day in Destin

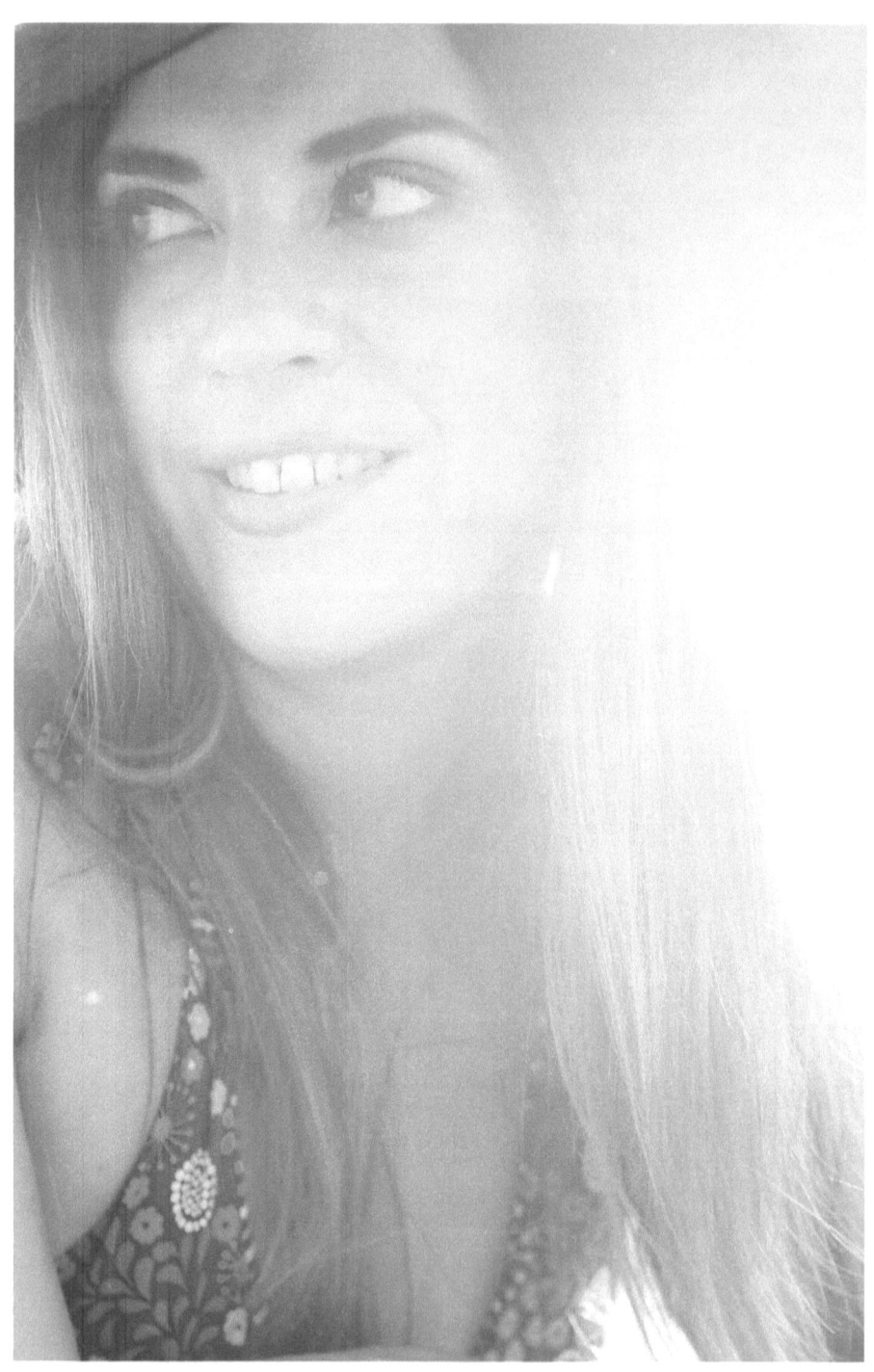

"SUNSHINE"

WHAT DO YOU BRING TO THE BEACH?
snacks, friends, music? what are your must haves?

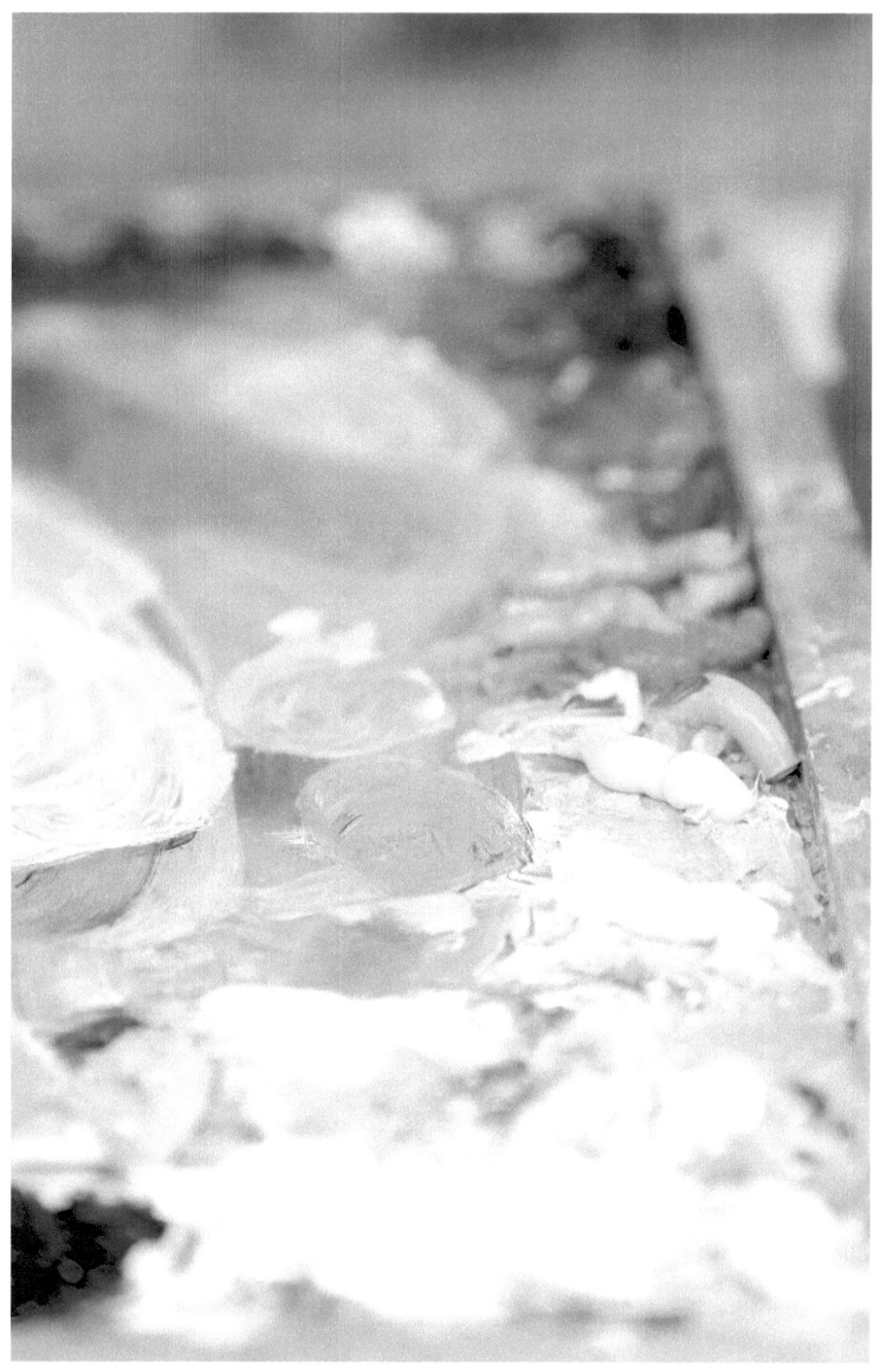

"TIME TO PAINT"

WHAT ARE YOUR FAVORITE COLORS?

find some colors and give it to the photo on the left

draw a paint brush and a tube of paint too

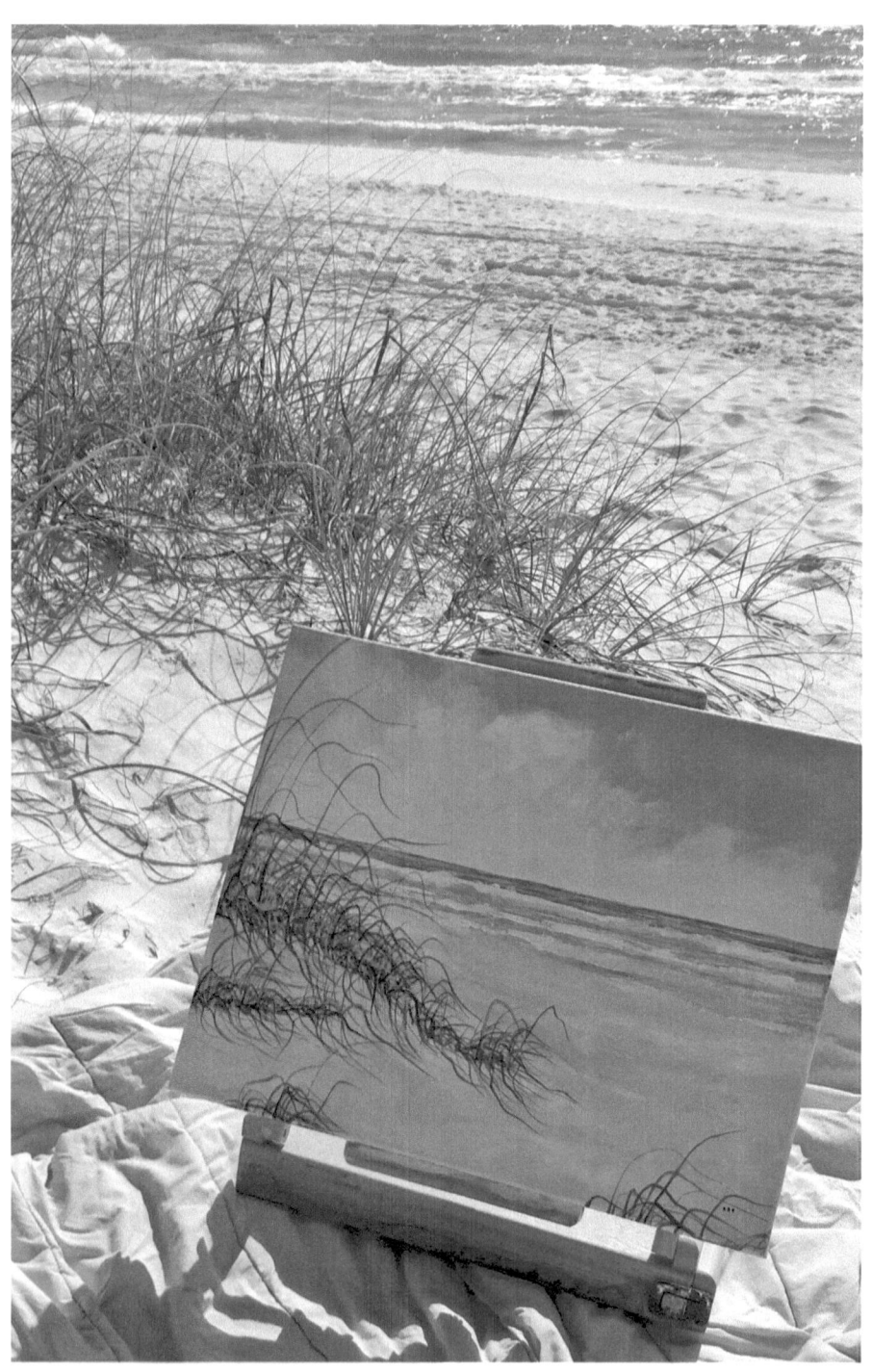

"EMERALD COAST PLEIN AIR PAINTING"

DO YOU LIKE TO...

draw, paint, write poems? let your creative side shine

_____

_____

_____

_____

_____

_____

_____

_____

_____

_____

_____

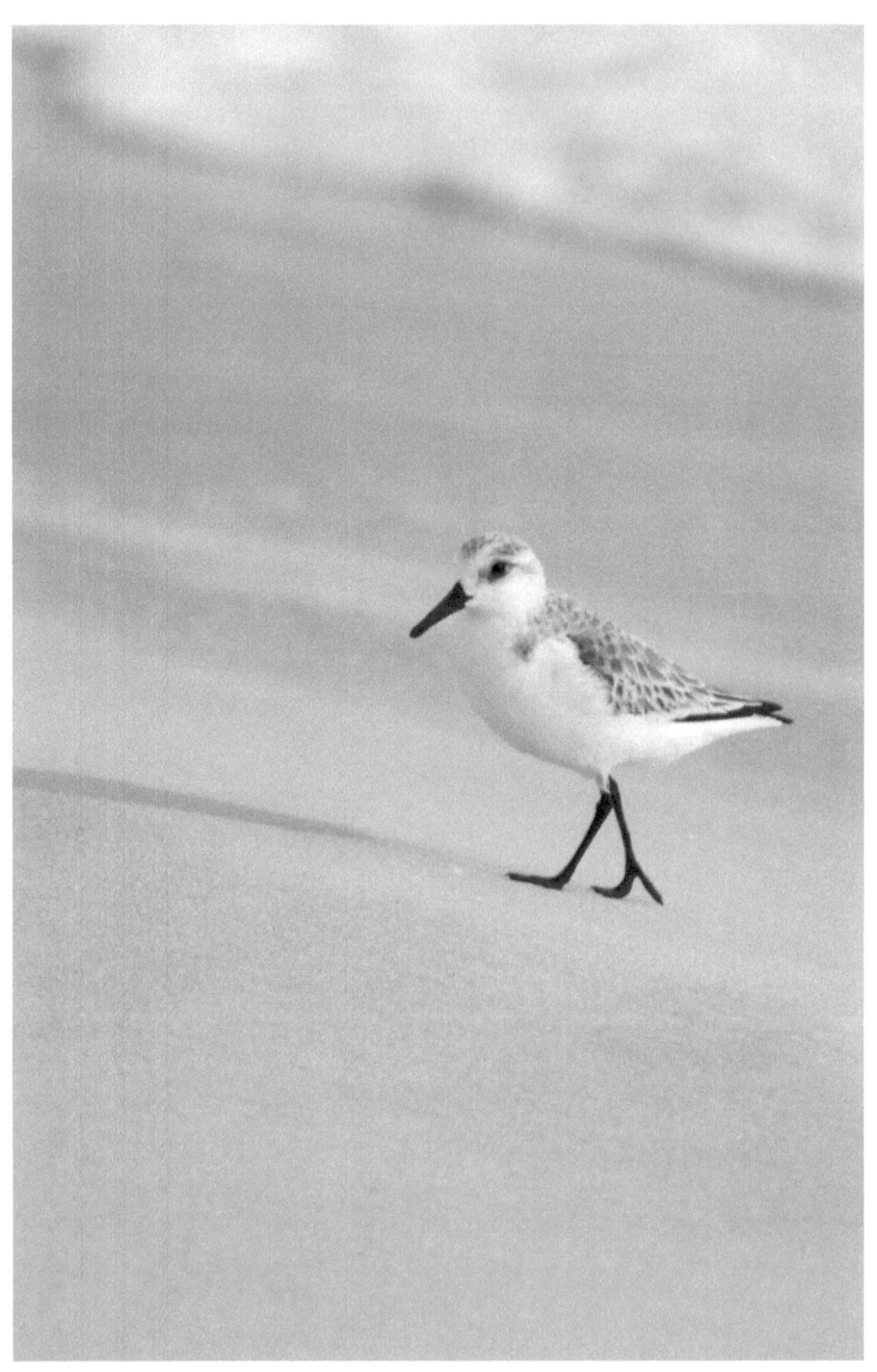

"THIS SANDPIPER IS CUTE"

WHAT MAKES YOU FASHIONABLE?
what accessory, scent, shirt or pair of jeans brings out your runway diva?

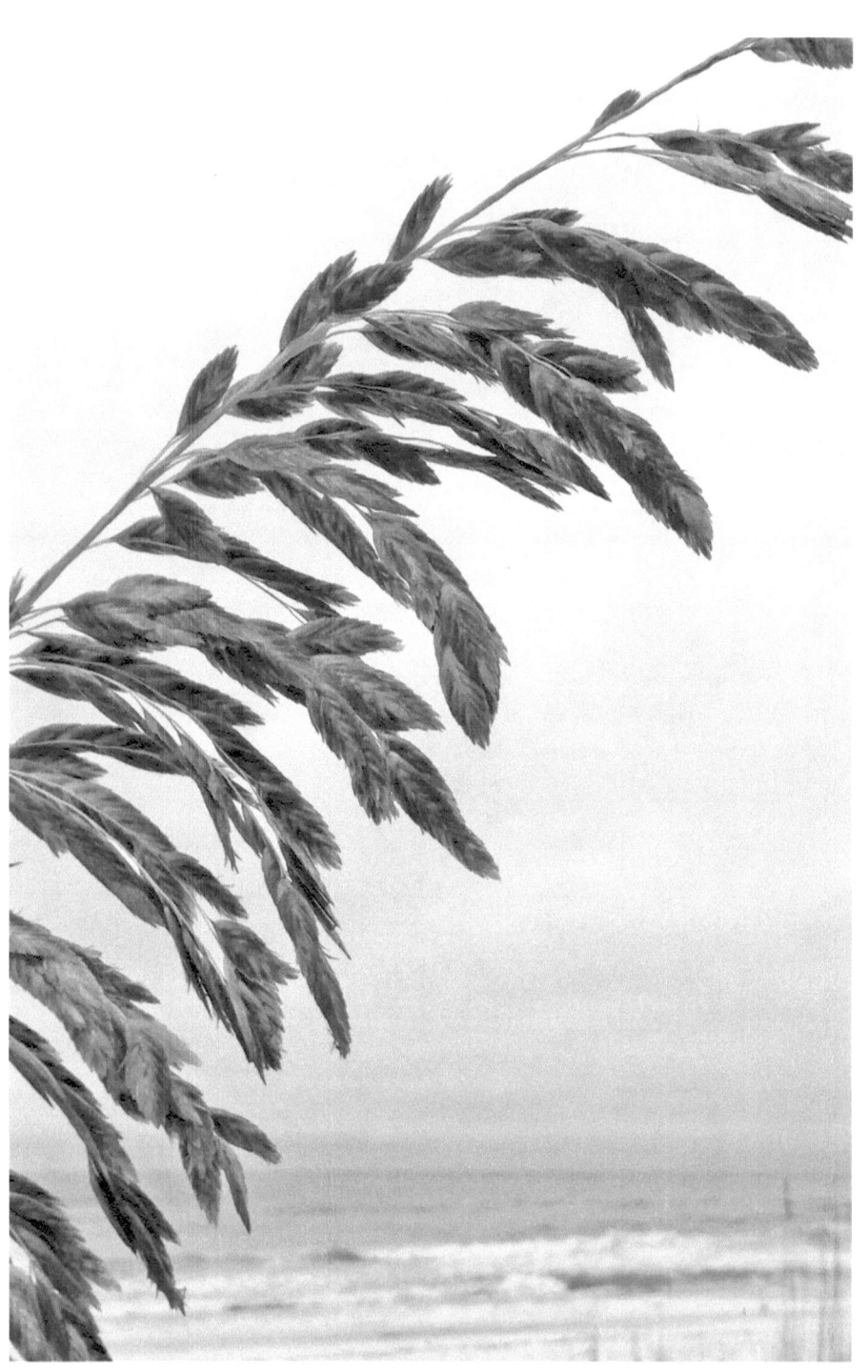

"DON'T PICK THE SEA OATS"

WHAT ARE YOUR STRONG INFLUENCES?

who or what has made a big influence in your life?

draw something strong even if it's just a bold word

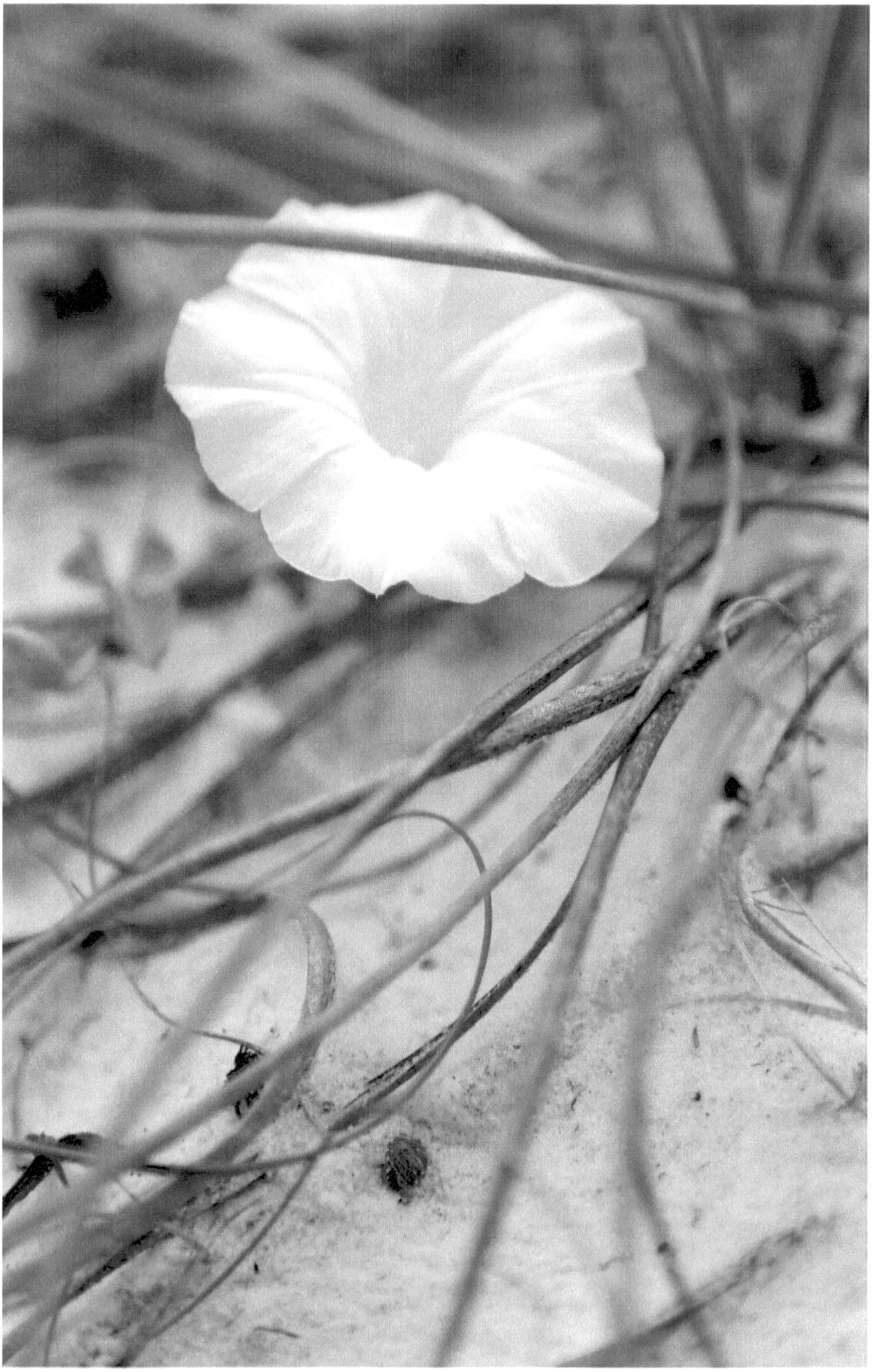

"A FLOWER BLOOMS"

WHAT IS BEAUTY?
where do you find it?

draw a flower with a bumble bee on the bottom of this page

_____

_____

_____

_____

_____

_____

_____

_____

_____

_____

"DESTIN BRIDGE AHEAD"

WHAT HAVE YOU HAD TO GET OVER?

I'm sure it has been more than just this bridge in Destin. write it down
and then draw a happy face because you did get over whatever it was

_____

_____

_____

_____

_____

_____

_____

_____

_____

_____

_____

_____

_____

_____

_____

_____

_____

_____

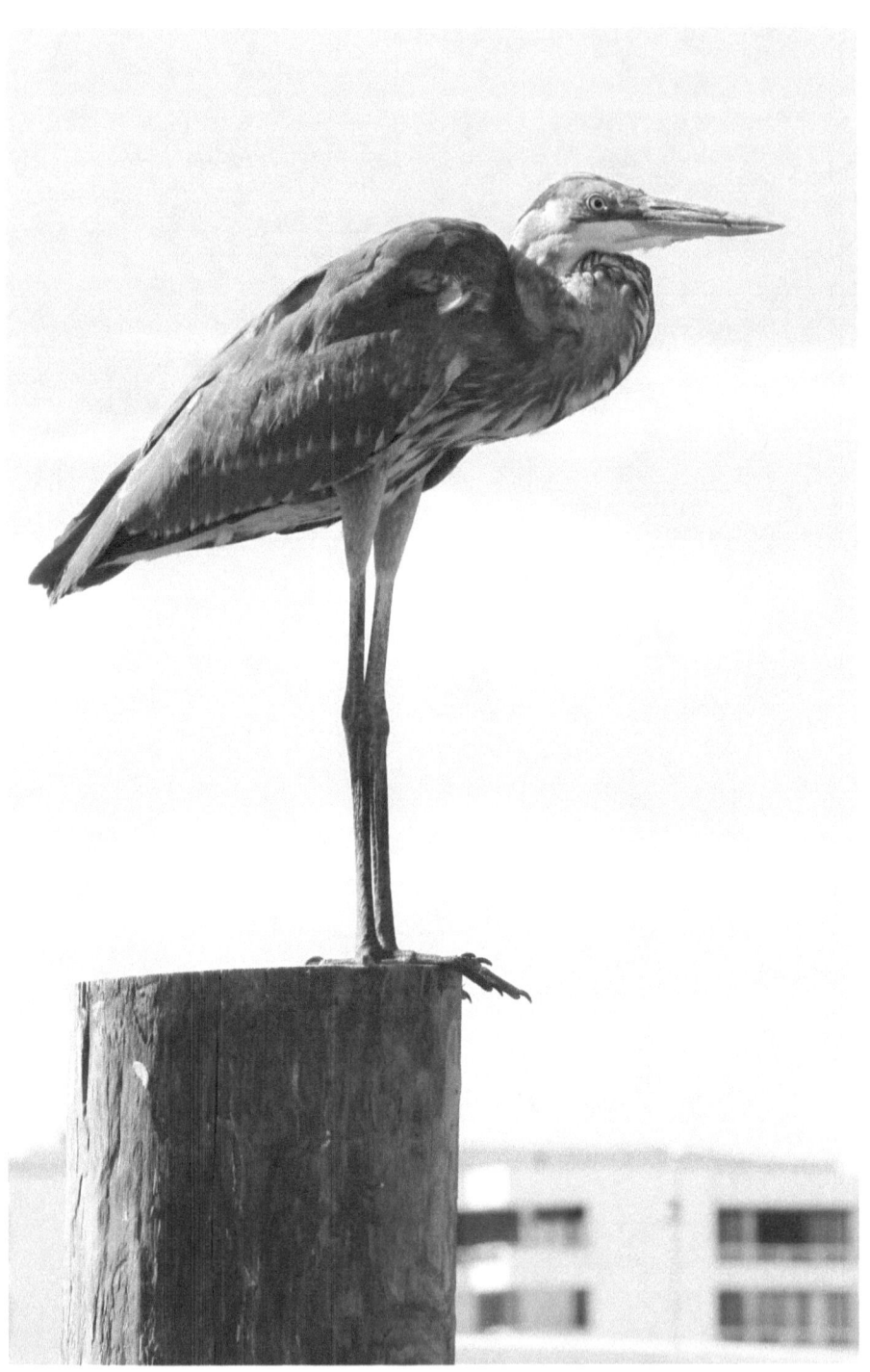

"WAITING FOR DINNER TO COME"

WHERE DO WE GO FROM HERE?
you're at the end of the pier or losing your mind... what's next?
tell the world and start writing it here

draw what your "crazy" face looks like at the bottom of the page

---

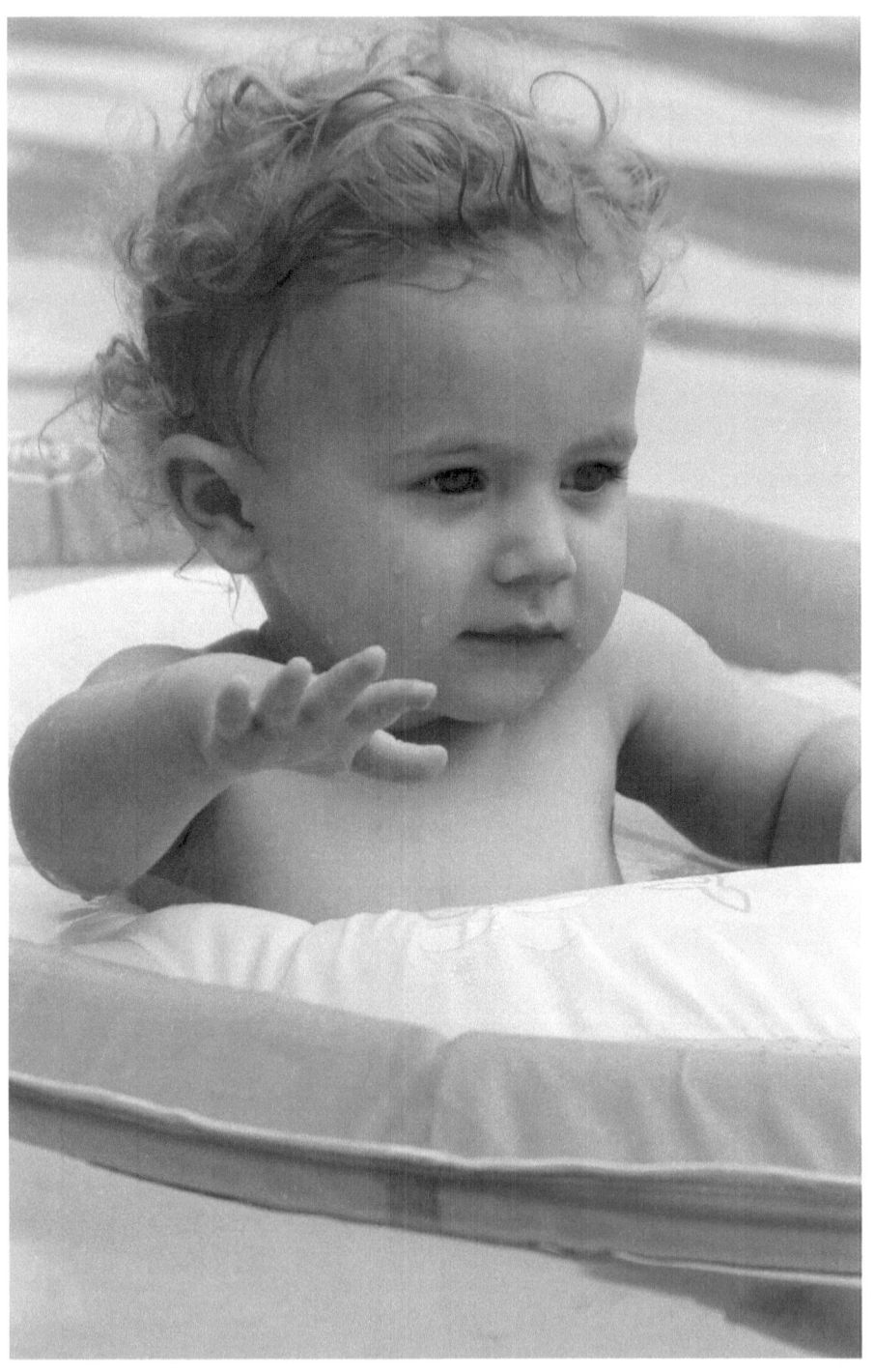

"IN THE POOL"

FAMILY FIRST

write a few lines about some of the people in your family

NORTHWEST FLORIDA... another day in Destin

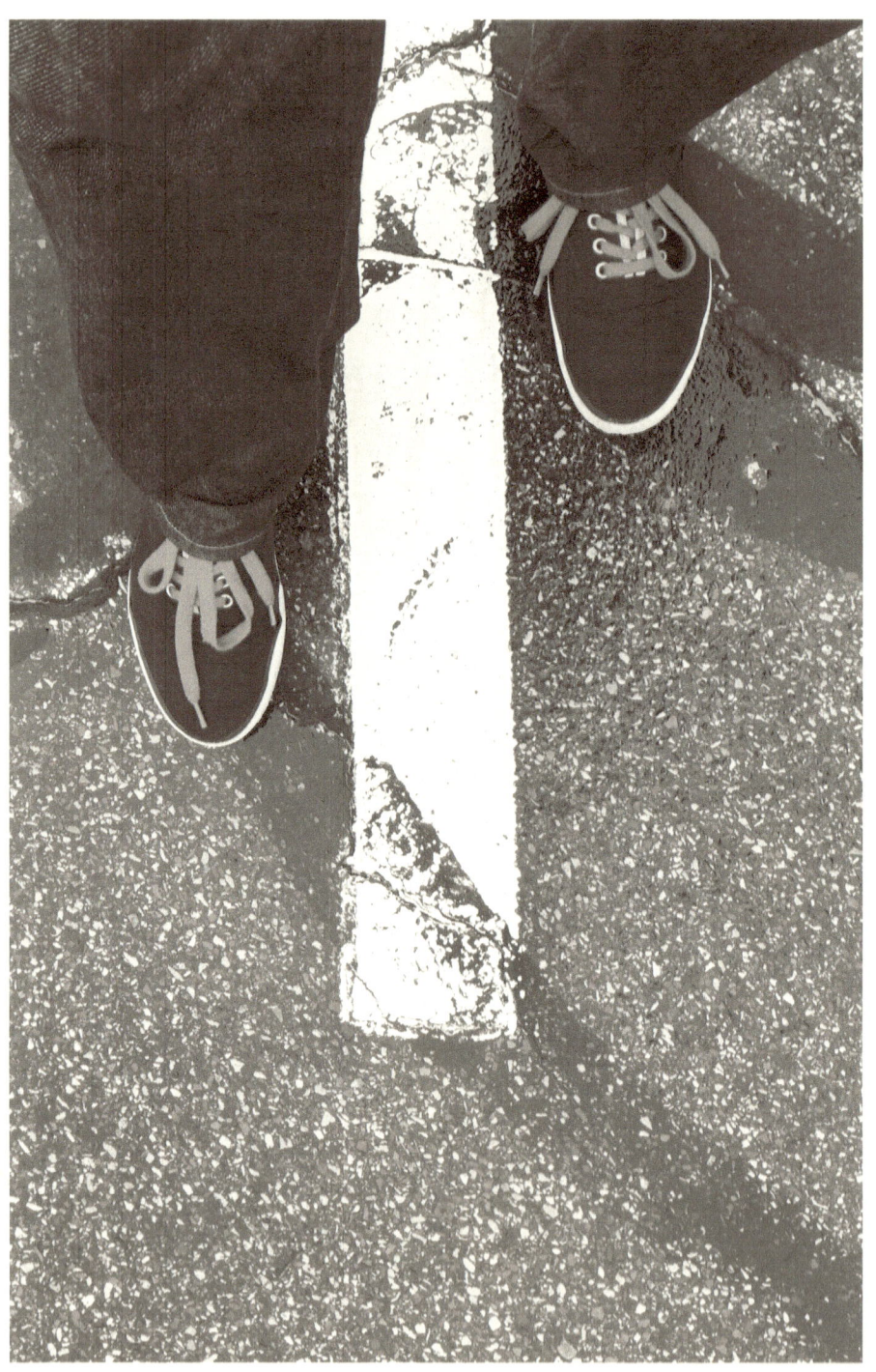

"THE LINE STOPS HERE"

WHAT'S NEXT?

the end of the book, well almost... what are you going to do now?
would you walk a mile in someone else's shoes? whose shoes?

_____

_____

_____

_____

_____

_____

_____

_____

_____

_____

_____

_____

_____

_____

_____

_____

_____

_____

_____

_____

_____

_____

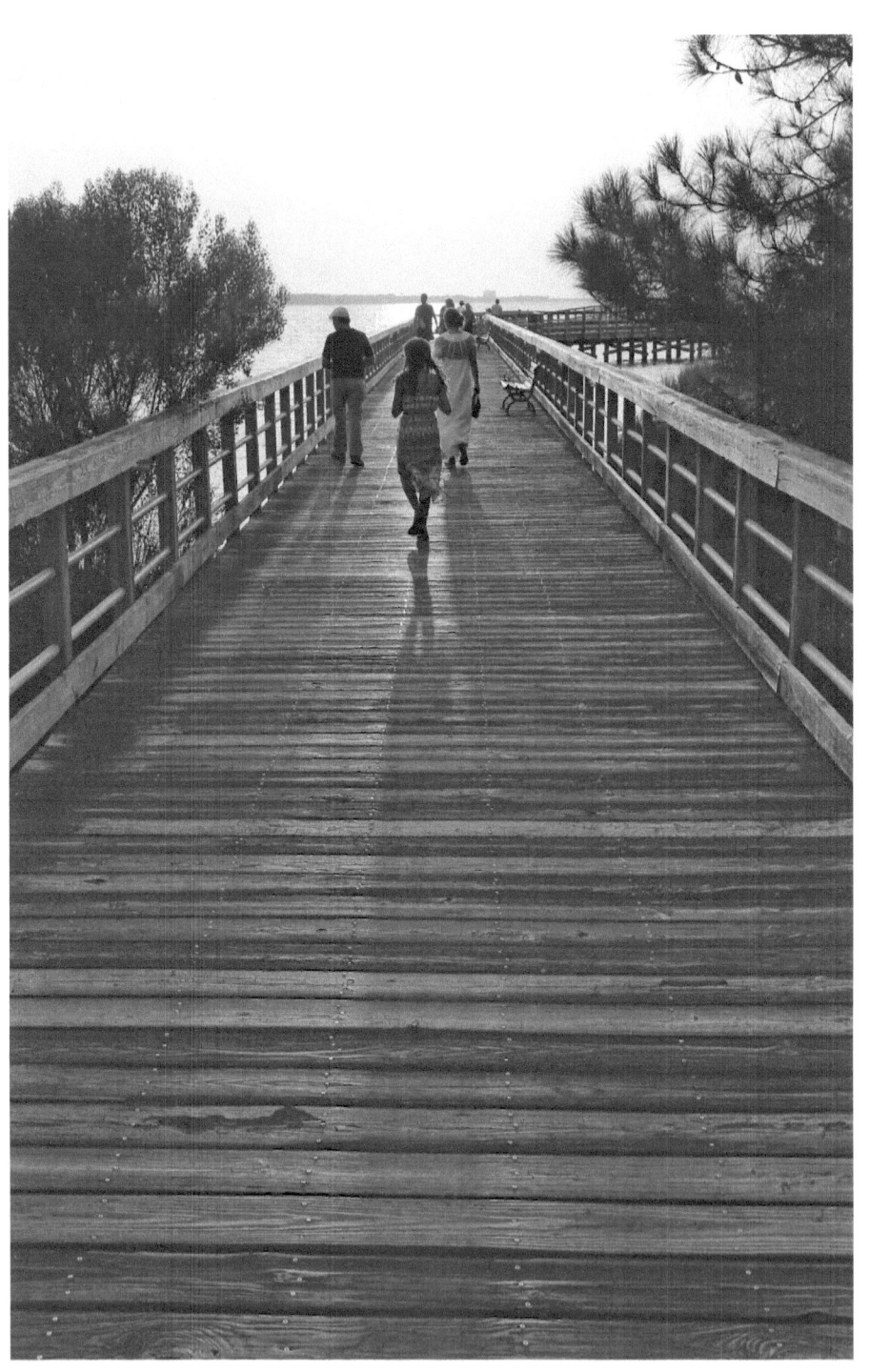

"SOUTH WALTON NEXT?"

DO YOU LIKE LINKS?

more stuff to look at, play with, and explore... write down some of the ones
you would like to remember when you get back home

for the ladies, a Destin fashion blog.........................www.wearindestin.com
Jim Clark's photography in color.................................destinartgallery.com
some Destin stuff ....www.cafepress.com/northwestflorida
advertising guy... www.juststay.com

NORTHWEST FLORIDA... another day in Destin